The Many Lives of Eddie Rickenbacker

The Many Lives of
Eddie Rickenbacker

Andrew Speno

BIOGRAPHIES FOR YOUNG READERS

Ohio University Press
Athens

Ohio University Press, Athens, Ohio 45701
ohioswallow.com
© 2020 by Andrew Speno

To obtain permission to quote, reprint, or otherwise reproduce or distribute
material from Ohio University Press publications, please contact our rights
and permissions department at (740) 593-1154 or (740) 593-4536 (fax).

Printed in the United States of America
Ohio University Press books are printed on acid-free paper ♾ ™

30 29 28 27 26 25 24 23 22 21 20   5 4 3 2 1

Frontispiece: Sergeant Edward Rickenbacker, 1917.
Photograph courtesy of Auburn University Libraries Special Collections and Archives

Hardcover ISBN: 978-0-8214-2430-8
Paperback ISBN: 978-0-8214-2431-5
Electronic ISBN: 978-0-8214-4722-2

Library of Congress Cataloging-in-Publication Data available upon request

For my grandfather, Richard K. Patrick:

It all started with you.

Contents

Author's Note

Someday It Will Be a Hundred Years Ago.

That's what my grandfather, Poppy, called the book he wrote in 1970. He was looking back sixty years to his childhood in the first decades of the twentieth century. At the same time, he was projecting ahead forty years into the twenty-first century, when he imagined his grown grandchildren would read his memoir and learn about his life a century before. Past and future all rolled up together.

In 2010, sixteen years after my grandfather's death, I read this book with the curious title, just as he had hoped I might. I discovered right away that Poppy was a good writer. He made me *feel* as I read his stories. I tensed up as he was dragged across his neighbors' field by their horse, Chelis. I felt his sadness when he had to go to the shed and butcher Henrietta, his favorite chicken. I laughed when he and his brother sold lemonade to Italian road-workers, only to see them spit it out as too sour. I was surprised when Poppy was reprimanded (in Morse code) by a ship's captain for using the navy's frequency on his homemade crystal radio set. I had expected a hundred years ago to be quaint and old-fashioned, but it seemed like an exciting time to be alive in Poppy's telling.

Of all his stories, the one about his family's first automobile trip might have sparked my imagination the most. After purchasing a used Model T Ford, his family all piled in, eager to drive to their annual summer vacation in Maine. All, that is, except Poppy's father, who worked for the railroad and wouldn't be caught dead in a motorcar.

The roads from Reading, Massachusetts, to Kennebunkport, Maine, were rough and indirect. "Often you drove twenty miles to advance only ten," my grandfather wrote. On this ill-fated trip the Ford went through *five* flat tires. The trip of a hundred miles took eleven hours. Poppy's father, who had left later by train, was waiting for the rest of the family at Uncle Charlie's when they finally arrived.

It must have been an exhausting trip, but it was exciting to read about. It sounded adventurous to me.

And so I developed a fascination for the early automobile. And in my research, I encountered a certain race-car driver by the name of Rickenbacker, who was described by a rival as "the most daring and **withal** [yet] the most cautious driver in America today."[1] Only later did I become interested in Eddie Rickenbacker the World War I fighter pilot (during my research I learned he was, again, both bold and careful).

When I discovered the Biographies for Young Readers series, I thought immediately of that auto racer and combat pilot from Columbus, who came of age when my grandfather was a boy. I thought about how he led the country in adopting both the automobile and the airplane. And I knew young readers would thrill to read about the adventures of this famous Ohioan, Eddie Rickenbacker.

So, here I am asking you, my reader, to do what my grandfather once asked of me: imagine the world of a hundred years ago in all its old-fashioned wonder. Consider how, for all the modern conveniences he lacked, Eddie was able to do things that you and I will never do. Fashion a new bearing at a blacksmith's shop in order to keep a lieutenant colonel's car running? Eddie did that. Fly a one-seater plane with the wind blowing in his goggled face? He did that, too. As you read, notice how, for all the hardship of his upbringing, he created opportunities for himself and built a life with more thrills, possibly, than a modern-day rollercoaster (and with almost as many twists and turns).

It was an exciting world a hundred years ago. Especially if you were a kid with grit and gumption . . . like Eddie Rickenbacker.

The Many Lives of Eddie Rickenbacker

BLACK SHEEP OF THE FAMILY

October 1890 to August 1904

"I was just a harum-scarum, wild, ruthless sort of kid."
—Eddie Rickenbacker[1]

WHEN HE was about twelve years old, Eddie Rickenbacker tried to "fly" a bike off a barn roof. Not so far away, the Wright Brothers were developing what would become the world's first self-powered aircraft. Eddie's flying machine was a little more primitive.

He found an old bike and removed the tires so the metal rims would speed down the corrugated metal roof. "Steel against steel," he said.[2] To the handlebars, he tied a large umbrella, the kind that street peddlers use to mount on their wagons. Eddie didn't know what would happen when he landed, but he and his partner, Sam Wareham, dumped a pile of sand below the eaves to break their fall, just in case. Sam would go second, but he never got his chance. The umbrella popped, Eddie crashed, and the bike was a total loss. Thanks to the sand pile, Eddie was just shaken up.

What kind of a kid rides an umbrella-bike off a twenty-five-foot roof?

One with a lot to prove, certainly. A boy grasping at greatness even at the risk of failure. The kid on the barn roof was more than a little reckless, but also smart enough to take precautions, just in case. He was, above all, unafraid of "learning the hard way," no matter the pain.[3] (And what could be more painful than a crash-landing from twenty-five feet?) That was the kind of boy Eddie Rickenbacker was. Those were the traits that shaped the kind of man he became.

Eddie Rickenbacker's disastrous first flight ended in a crash-landing, but it did not stop him from becoming a giant in the field of **aviation** when he grew up. That first flight might have killed him, but it was just one of dozens of crack-ups, near misses, and brushes with death that marked his long and productive life. It would be a life so full and so often saved from disaster, one could be forgiven for thinking it was many, many more than just one.

Edward Rickenbacker was born October 8, 1890, in Columbus, Ohio, the third of eight children of William and Lizzie Rickenbacher. Mary and Bill came before Eddie, who was followed by Emma, Luise (dead before her third birthday), Louis, Dewey, and Albert. His parents started their lives as Wilhelm Rickenbacher and Liesl Basler in the German-speaking region of northwest Switzerland. Each, separately, emigrated to America for opportunity. Liesl sought independence from a large, confining family. Wilhelm dreamed of starting his own construction business. Each chose Columbus because of its large German-speaking population. To better fit into their adopted country, they Americanized their first names to William and Lizzie.

(Years later, during the war with Germany, Eddie changed the spelling of his last name. He swapped the "h" for a second "k" to make it appear less German. For clarity, this book will use the spelling Rickenbacker later adopted, even when writing about his earlier years.)

In Columbus, Lizzie and William met, married, and built a family together in their own home, two miles southeast of downtown. "The little house on Livingston Avenue,"[4] as Eddie called it, was the end of

The Rickenbacker house at 1334 Livingston Avenue. The rear addition, built by Eddie's father, made the "little house" a little less little.
Courtesy of Auburn University Libraries Special Collections and Archives

the line at that time, the outer limits of the city. No pavement covered the street. No gas or running water reached the inside of its walls—certainly no electricity did. The Rickenbacker home was surrounded by empty lots and scattered houses which gave way, on the south and east, to farmland all the way to the horizon and beyond.

Alas, William's American Dream kept slipping from his grasp. More than once, he tried to start his own business, but each time it failed. In and out of a handful of brewery and building jobs, he remained a **wage laborer**. Lizzie took in laundry to add to their income, but hard times were the Rickenbackers' "constant companions," as Lizzie put it.[5] They made do with little and grew or raised what they could not buy with money. The children all chipped in. They hoed and weeded the garden, harvested its potatoes, cabbages, and turnips. They picked grapes from

3

THE GERMANS OF COLUMBUS

TWO GERMAN IMMIGRANTS were among the first residents of the newly established Ohio state capital in 1812. Tens of thousands more Germans came to Columbus during the next four decades. They established German-language newspapers, German-language public schools, German breweries, and more. By midcentury roughly one-third of the city's population was of German heritage. The fraction would never again be as large. By the time Eddie went to school in the 1890s, German-language instruction in elementary schools was being cut back. When the United States went to war against Germany in 1917, all German culture in Columbus was actively rejected.

After the First World War, *Die Alte Sud Ende*, the Old South End, went into decline. Two-thirds of the buildings were demolished to make room for new development. But in 1959, a forward-thinking group of investors began buying up neglected properties and restoring them. The City of Columbus joined the effort, and in 1963, by law, created the German Village Historic District.

Visit German Village today and tour the narrow brick streets and quaint brick homes that look much as they did in Eddie Rickenbacker's day. Try Schmidt's Sausage Haus for authentic German food—and don't forget to order the half-pound Jumbo Cream Puff, in one of four flavors, for dessert!

the vines, gathered eggs from the chickens in the "barn."[6] Eddie looked after the goats, staking them in empty lots to graze.

He learned to **hustle** for other things the family needed, or he wanted. Sometimes that meant stealing. There was an especially good walnut tree on a farm down Alum Creek. He and his big brother, Bill, would go down with a sack and, like squirrels, stock up for winter. Once

Liesl "Lizzie" Basler about the time of her wedding, 1885 Courtesy of Auburn University Libraries Special Collections and Archives

Eddie fell from a high branch and was "knocked senseless . . . for about an hour."[7] Other times, the brothers scrounged coal dropped along the tracks or swiped it from coal cars. Twice Eddie was almost run over by a switching car but was rescued at the last second by Bill.

More often, hustling meant working as many odd jobs as he could find: setting up pins at the local bowling alley; delivering papers for the *Columbus Dispatch*; hauling jugs of water and beer to farm workers; collecting rags, bones, and scrap metal to sell to the junkman. Eddie insisted he didn't mind the work. He called it "a privilege."[8]

School was mostly not a privilege. Classmates mocked his German accent, calling him "Dutchy" or "Kraut."[9] One year, they ridiculed his mismatched shoes: brown and rounded on one foot, yellow and pointed on the other.

"As far as my studies were concerned," Eddie said, "I had no trouble with them. The only difficulty I had was because of the mischief I got into."[10] He said he got into a lot of fights and **played hooky** whenever he could get away with it (and even when he couldn't). He was "sort of the leader"[11] of the Horsehead Gang, which took its name from the sign on the local horse track, called the Driving Park, down the street. The gang built a tree house of scavenged lumber where they hung out and smoked cigarettes, undisturbed by adults. One time, the gang went up and down Miller Avenue breaking streetlamps, like common **hoodlums**. William gave Eddie a severe thrashing when the police showed up at the door. Another time, they took rides on a loading cart down the tracks at the local gravel pit. The cart ran over Eddie's leg and gave him a serious gash.

Mr. and Mrs. Rickenbacker worried about Eddie's misbehavior. "You'll wind up in **reformatory** and be a jailbird," they warned.[12] William beat him, in frustration. Lizzie wept, in desperation.

Young Eddie began to think of himself as "the black sheep of the family,"[13] but he was not only that. He had a sensitive side, too. He was, he said, "crazy about painting watercolors," and "particularly fond of flowers and scenery and animals."[14] He developed a crush on a girl in Sunday school and painted pictures for her. He was "sweet on" his third-grade teacher, Miss Alexander, too. In the spring, he brought her flowers picked from neighbors' gardens on the way to school: tulips, lilacs, and peonies, each kind as it came into season. In time, Miss Alexander grew suspicious, and the neighbors began to complain. Eddie received two thrashings for his thievery, one at school and one at home.[15]

Eddie showed a creative side, too, and a budding interest in speed. He and his friends designed "push-mobiles"[16] out of discarded boards and baby carriage wheels. They laid out a large dirt track and held races. And, of course, he designed an umbrella-bike to "fly" off a barn roof. It didn't work the way he planned, but at least it showed he was thinking.

Unknown to young Eddie, trouble was brewing in his world—trouble more serious than any he and his friends could think up. After years of trying to become his own boss, William remained a common

Eddie (*on the right*) with Sam Wareham, his partner in the umbrella-bike stunt
(Where did they get those military uniforms?)
Courtesy of Auburn University Libraries Special Collections and Archives

2

MAN OF THE HOUSE

August 1904 to Summer 1906

*"Since that time, I have been completely on my own . . . ,
taking the hard knocks and making the best of it."*
—Eddie Rickenbacker[1]

EDDIE WAS determined to replace his father's lost income. His sister Mary, eighteen years old, and brother Bill, seventeen, worked full-time at a clothing factory across town, but he was the next oldest. He would do his part to keep his family out of poverty. No longer would he be the black sheep of the family. Now, in his own mind at least, he would be the "man of the house."

Introducing himself to a potential employer, Eddie looked suspiciously young—too young to be hired legally. But Eddie fudged and said he was already fourteen and an eighth-grade graduate. The man never questioned him. He was pleased to get an eager youngster, willing to work long hours for short wages. Eddie knew it, too, so when the job didn't meet his expectations, he quit and tried another. He tried five different jobs in the next twelve months.

Federal Glass Company was exhausting and dangerous. (He hauled heavy trays of hot glasses all night long.) Buckeye Steel Castings Com-

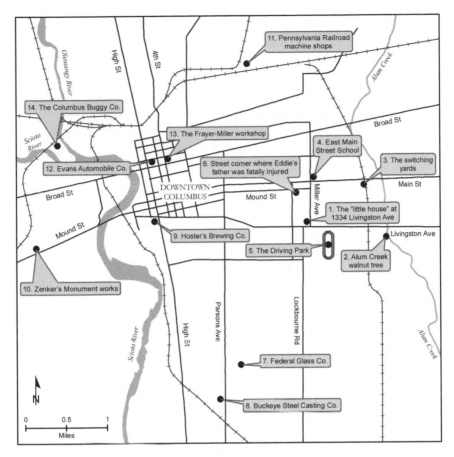

Eddie's Columbus, 1890–1907.
Courtesy of Brian Balsley

pany was messy. (Sand from the molds kept getting in his hair and clothes.) Hoster Brewing Company was repetitive and smelly. (He capped bottles of beer, breathing the smell of stale **hops**.)

Eddie worked ten to twelve hours a day, six days a week, for no more than a dollar a day (which would be worth about thirty dollars today). He walked as much as six miles round trip to save nickels on trolley fare. Only later, with his family getting back on its feet, did Eddie use his savings to buy a bike. And—somehow—he saved money for painting lessons. He began to dream of a career as an artist.

Eddie helped carve the headstone for his father's grave at Green Lawn Cemetery.
Courtesy of Auburn University Libraries Special Collections and Archives

But it was all dream and no reality. So he took up an engraving apprenticeship at Zenker Monument Works. If he could not be a painter, he decided, he would be a kind of sculptor instead. Eddie learned enough from Mr. Zenker to engrave the lettering of his father's headstone. He carved a stone Bible as a gift for his mother, too. But dust from the stone grinding gave him a cough, and Lizzie was concerned. Tuberculosis, a disease of the lungs, had killed some in her family. Eddie had sworn never to worry his mother. He quit Zenker's without hesitation.

Now sixteen, Eddie found his next job across town at the Pennsylvania Railroad machine shop. There, he discovered that machines could satisfy his artistic interests, too. Working the **lathe**, Eddie explained, "You are again making something with your hands, . . . carving out a piece of beautiful machinery from a piece of rough steel."[2] Eddie might well have become a **machinist**, but a freak accident changed the course of his history. A wheel fell off a passing handcart, causing it to tip and dump its load of heavy timbers. The falling wood slammed Eddie against his lathe, giving him a bad set of cuts and bruises. His boss sent him home to recover.

Confined to his bed several days, Eddie pondered the direction his life was taking. He thought of the automobiles beginning to appear on Columbus's streets. He remembered the Ford salesman, standing on a street corner, drawing a crowd to view his Model A and then—oh, the joy!—giving Eddie a ride in it. Railroads were the transportation of the past. Automobiles represented the promise of the future. There was no question but that Eddie would throw in his lot with the future.

When he recovered enough to walk, Eddie went downtown to Evans Automobile Company. Formerly a bicycle repairman, Mr. Evans now provided garage service, storage and upkeep, for three motorcars. One was steam powered, another gas powered, and a third electrical. Eddie wheedled a job out of Mr. Evans and never went back to the Pennsylvania Railroad.

It wasn't glamorous work. He repaired bicycles, replaced tubes and tires, built and charged batteries—and took a large pay cut, besides. But it was worth it to Eddie just to be near those glorious new machines. Besides, when Mr. Evans was away, on business or at home, Eddie gave himself a special **fringe benefit**: a spin in one of the motorcars. Just around the garage, at first, bumping it a few feet forward and a few feet back in the cramped garage. It was his secret. Mr. Evans never had to know.

But the boss might well have found out on the day Eddie allowed the two-cylinder Packard to run out of oil. The **pistons** seized up in their chambers, and the engine looked to be a goner. Desperate, Eddie opened up the crankcase and pried the cylinders free with a crowbar. Then he refilled the oil, restarted the motor, and parked the car in its place.[3] Crisis avoided, barely.

From the first day, Frayer watched his new errand boy "like a hawk."[3] He was surprised to catch him reading papers over lunch. Eddie explained that he had signed up for a correspondence course in automotive engineering. Each month he would receive a new lesson in the mail, study the material, complete the assignments, and mail them back to be graded. For a second time in the week, Frayer was impressed. Here was a kid with gumption—and ambition. He gave Eddie more responsibility.

GOOD TIMING

In 1906 the Frayer-Miller company provided the perfect time and place for Eddie to learn automotive engineering. It was still a craftsmen's workshop. There was no **assembly line**. There were no standardized parts. The men worked together to build one car at a time, from the ground up. They used machine tools to craft all the parts: every rod, cam, gear, and valve. If one didn't fit, they filed it down until it did. If the machinery failed to meet their standards, they went back to the drawing board and changed the design. Eddie was involved in almost every step of the process.

Frayer-Miller was no ordinary automobile workshop, either. The men were building three race cars to enter in the famous Vanderbilt Cup race in New York. When the day came to head east, Frayer invited Eddie to come along. The hard-working **apprentice** would be his riding mechanic during the three-hundred-mile road race. He would sit next to Frayer, checking the gauges, monitoring the wear on the tires, and looking out for drivers coming from behind—all this while bouncing over unpaved roads at speeds up to eighty miles an hour and taking unbanked turns with no seatbelt to hold him in. The roar of the primitive engine would drown out even his loudest shouts, so Eddie would communicate with Frayer by hand signals. Two taps to the shoulder meant *Pull over; a tire is about to blow.* One tap on the thigh meant *Move over; we're being passed.*

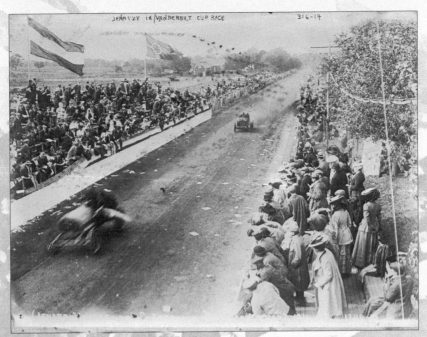

Camille Jenatzy and Arthur Duray race through the crowd at the 1906 Vanderbilt Cup race.
Library of Congress Prints and Photographs Division: LC-DIG-ggbain-01457

THE GLORIOUS (AND WILD) VANDERBILT CUP RACES OF 1904–1910

WILLIAM VANDERBILT, the thrill-seeking grandson of America's "first **tycoon**,"[4] Cornelius Vanderbilt, established the Vanderbilt Cup road race in 1904. Safety was a concern from the beginning. New York spectators muscled their way onto the road to get a better look. More than a few close calls resulted. One spectator was killed and two boys injured in 1906, the year when Eddie and Frayer failed to qualify. The deaths of two mechanics and hospitalization of twenty-two spectators in 1910 ended the Vanderbilt Cup races on Long Island roadways.

The team of Frayer and Rickenbacker took two unpromising practice runs and had a disastrous qualifying race. Their engine overheated badly, and, no matter how hard Eddie pumped oil, the temperature gauge kept rising. Black smoke spewed from the engine. The pistons banged like sledgehammers. Frayer turned off the ignition and pulled to a stop. Eddie felt the sting of failure, but Frayer understood that defeat was all in the game. He taught Eddie the first lesson of sportsmanship: *Try your hardest to win, but don't cry if you lose.*[5]

UNCOMMON TALENT

Back in Columbus, Frayer took a new job with a bigger company, a bigger paycheck, and a new challenge: to pull a successful horse-drawn carriage company into the Motor Age. It would be his job to design the company's first modern gasoline-powered automobile. He accepted the job on the condition that his young assistant come with him.

Just like that, seventeen-year-old Eddie became chief testing engineer at Columbus Buggy Company. Now he was supervising twelve grown men, some of them twice his age. As supervisor, he wore a necktie under the bib of his overalls. As engineer, he made two-dimensional drawings for craftsmen to build into actual parts. As product tester— and this was the fun part—he drove the new models on tours through the city and into the countryside. On one tour, the brakes failed the test going down a hill. The car wrecked, but Eddie walked away with just a few bruises. Not for the first time—and certainly not the last—luck was on his side.

Eddie was getting to know the working of motors, inside and out. He was learning, he said, to "speak the language of the **internal combustion" engine**.[6] One day his budding talent got noticed by a man possibly even more important to him than Lee Frayer.

Columbus Buggy president Clinton Firestone liked to take the scenic route to work. On this day, his motorcar broke down north of town, and he called the factory for help. Frayer turned to Eddie and

said, "The Old Man is stuck at the storage dam. Go up and fix him up." Eddie did as he was told, but when he approached, Firestone hesitated. "I asked for a man, not a kid," he grumbled.[7] Eddie stayed cool and lifted the hood. He had the problem fixed before you could say "Firestone-Columbus," the name of the new Frayer-designed car. For a second time, Mr. Firestone was taken aback. This kid knew engines as well as any man—maybe better. Like Frayer before him, Firestone took a keen interest in Eddie's career.

Whenever he needed a man for a special assignment, Firestone turned to his eighteen-year-old testing engineer. Columbus Buggy's old model, the high wheeler that still looked more like a buggy than an automobile, wouldn't climb the dunes for Atlantic City drivers. So Firestone sent Eddie east to investigate. The new Frayer-designed car

Eddie (*at the wheel*) drives three-time presidential candidate William Jennings Bryan (*directly behind Rickenbacker*) in his Firestone-Columbus. Notice the steering wheel on the right side. American automobiles had not yet settled on the left side as standard.
Courtesy of Auburn University Libraries Special Collections and Archives

was going to be introduced at the 1909 Chicago Automobile Show. The boss chose Eddie to be its driver and demonstrator. The Firestone-Columbus made a hit at the show but then kept overheating for customers in Dallas. So Firestone sent Eddie south to solve the problem. It took several days and a stroke of luck, but Eddie eventually did find the solution. When he wired back the news, Firestone instructed him to stay where he was. He wanted Eddie to oversee his **agency** selling Firestone-Columbuses in Texas.

LEARNING ON THE JOB

Just like that, eighteen-year-old Eddie became "salesman, demonstrator, mechanic, chief engineer, experimenter—in short, the whole ball of wax," he said.[8] There was no one to tell him what to do or how to do

Gone are the overalls: Eddie, age nineteen, is moving up in the world.
Courtesy of Auburn University Libraries Special Collections and Archives

it. He had to learn these jobs by doing them. When a famous presidential candidate, William Jennings Bryan, came to town, Eddie offered to be his **chauffeur**. He got his picture—and his *car's*—in the paper. The publicity brought him three sales the next day.

His next assignment was in Omaha, Nebraska. Firestone made Eddie branch manager in charge of six salesmen, selling automobiles in four states. He was no longer a skinny kid but a strapping six-foot-tall young man. "My, they must grow them big in Texas," Lizzie said when Eddie passed through on his way west.[9] He was earning enough now—more than most doctors or lawyers—to pay off the bank loan on his mother's house.[10] Now he really *was* the "man of the house." He really *was* moving up in the world.

But motorcars were still a hard sell in 1910, especially in the upper Midwest. They were useless in the snow and mud that dominated half the year. They broke down often, and there were too few mechanics to fix them. There weren't even any gas stations yet. Farmers and doctors were sticking with what they knew best: the horse. So how was Eddie going to convince them to buy a Firestone-Columbus automobile?

By racing it around a half-mile dirt oval, of course.

DID YOU KNOW?

Columbus was once the buggy capital of the world. Columbus Buggy Company went into the carriage business in 1875 and by 1892 was building more than three hundred thousand horse-drawn vehicles a year. It was not the only buggy maker in the city, though. Some believe that in 1900, about one in six buggies *worldwide* were made in Columbus, Ohio.

KING OF THE
DIRT-TRACK RACERS

June 1910 to January 1917

"I had more lead in my feet than brains in my head."
—Eddie Rickenbacker[1]

Auto racing, Henry Ford believed, "brought advertising of the only kind that people cared to read." Automobile salesmen in the early twentieth century agreed. "Win on Sunday, sell on Monday"—that was their motto.[2]

The key was to win on Sunday (or Saturday, as the case might be). So Eddie adapted his Firestone-Columbus touring car for the racetrack. He removed the fenders, reinforced the frame, attached an extra gas tank, and painted the body white. Then he crossed the river to Red Oak, Iowa, for his first twenty-five-mile race. The night before, he practiced driving on the dirt track, "taking the turn at each end faster and faster, braking here, accelerating there," until he knew precisely the maximum speed he could use on each point of the track.[3] Eddie Rickenbacker was leaving nothing to chance.

Chance intervened anyway. His right rear tire blew out on a turn, and he smashed through the outer fence. His second race, like his first, ended in disappointment.

Although he was obsessed with neatness all his life, Eddie didn't mind getting dirty on the track. Courtesy of Auburn University Libraries Special Collections and Archives

Eddie picked himself up, fixed up his car, and went back out on the county-fair **circuit**. It wasn't long before he won. And won again. In fact, Eddie won more often than not that summer of 1910. At the Ak-sar-ben Festival at the end of the season (Aksarben is "Nebraska" spelled backwards), Eddie won five of the six races he entered.

It didn't matter how many times he won, though. At the end of each weekend Eddie had to return to the agency in Omaha to sell automobiles. He would rather have been spending his days building a better race car. "I started to get fed up and disgusted," Eddie said of his sales work.[4] So he bided his time until May 1911, when his **mentor**, Lee Frayer, invited him to be his relief driver at an exciting new event: the Indianapolis 500. Eddie drove the middle miles of the race, giving Frayer a rest in the seven-hour event, and helped him finish in a respectable thirteenth place.

Now Eddie was hooked. After racing on the bricks of the Indianapolis Motor Speedway, there was no going back to automobile sales in Omaha. He "wanted to drive good cars fast" and test his "automobile knowledge and driving skill and plain old guts against the world's

THE STORY OF THE BRICKYARD AND THE INDIANAPOLIS 500

THE INDIANAPOLIS MOTOR SPEEDWAY began as a dream—and almost ended in tragedy. Its hastily built crushed-limestone track led to three deaths and many injuries in its inaugural three-hundred-mile race in 1909. For his do-over, Speedway owner Carl Fisher hired two dozen workers to lay down 3,200,000 bricks, giving the track the sturdiest, most expensive surface available. After the first five-hundred-mile race in 1911, the Speedway earned the nickname the Brickyard. The bricks stayed in place until 1937 when the next owner (spoiler alert: his name was Rickenbacker) replaced them with asphalt.

best."[5] Eddie traded his $150-a-week sales position for a $3-a-day gig with the best race-car engineers in the state of Iowa, Fred and Augie Duesenberg. The brothers were building a race car to win on the AAA circuit, the American Automobile Association's professional racing league. Any prize money Eddie won along the way got invested right back into the Duesenberg enterprise.

In the spring of 1914, both money and time were running out. The Duesenberg team needed a win, or they would have to find real jobs that paid real money. They needed a win so badly they adopted a good luck charm, a black cat they called Lady Luck. Eddie put Lady Luck in a box behind his seat at the Indianapolis 500, but he still finished tenth and out of the money.

So, it was do or die at Sioux City on the Fourth of July.

Before the race, Eddie visited his mother in Columbus, and Lizzie pulled out her little book of Swiss legends. Inside, she found instructions for a good luck charm. She told her son to tie a bat's heart to his middle finger with a red silk thread. Then, good fortune would follow him throughout the race. Eddie was desperate enough to give it a try.

Eddie said engines talked to him. Here he is listening.
Courtesy of Ohio History Connection (AL02936.tif)

When the race day came, Eddie drove for all he was worth. He took the turns "at the top maximum speed for safety and perhaps a little bit more."[6] Holding the wheel steady for three hundred miles, with the bat's heart tied to his middle finger, required all the strength and endurance he could muster. A chunk of dirt track "gumbo" struck his mechanic and knocked him out for a few laps, but he and Eddie pulled through.[7] They crossed the finish ahead of all challengers and forty seconds before their next closest rival. Eddie's hard driving—with *maybe* a little help from Lizzie's superstition—had triumphed.

Another Duesenberg car won third place, so the team earned $12,500 in all. They would survive to race another day.

Ever resourceful, Eddie invented this set of masks by which driver and mechanic could communicate over the roar of the engines. They worked fine but were "unbearably hot and itchy."[8] Eddie tossed them after one use.
Courtesy of Auburn University Libraries Special Collections and Archives

But success created new challenges. Other teams began recruiting Eddie, and he faced a difficult decision: stick with his friends at Duesenberg or move on to bigger and better things. For Eddie, the "opportunity to gain knowledge of the different engineers and types of automobiles" was irresistible.[9] He drove the French-made Peugeot briefly but ultimately joined the American Maxwell team. Eddie Rickenbacker was no longer a weekend dirt-track racer. He was a national figure, competing against the best in the sport in races from coast to coast. At the end of 1915, he finished fifth in the AAA standings.

Eddie became known for his "reckless daring"[10] on the track. While other drivers kept their eyes on a stopwatch, one magazine wrote, Eddie drove "with his eyes on the car ahead of him."[11] Rickenbacker explained

Rickenbacker and his mechanic in their Maxwell Special on the bricks at Indianapolis Motor Speedway
Courtesy of Auburn University Libraries Special Collections and Archives

his approach this way: "It was confidence; nothing more than confidence. I was as strong as a bull in those days."[12]

Race car driving—maintaining eighty- and ninety-mile-per-hour speeds for one hundred, three hundred, or five hundred miles, whether on dirt, board, concrete, or brick track—was as physically and mentally demanding as any sport ever devised. One lapse in judgment, one distracted moment, could lead to death, not simply for oneself and one's mechanic, but for other drivers or even spectators. Before every race, Eddie's crew wrapped him up like a mummy, "from armpit to thigh," to keep him from being "shaken apart" by the vibrations.[13]

Eddie pushed his cars as hard as he pushed himself. Some said too hard. Certainly, he suffered his share of breakdowns and accidents. Yet Lady Luck, cat or no cat, stayed by his side. He always walked away more or less unharmed.

Eddie pushed his Maxwell team hard, too. Four mechanics and three drivers worked from early in the morning until late at night maintaining and improving their Maxwell Specials. To energize the men, Eddie bought a **Victrola** and a stack of records to play music in the shop. He wrote out rules of behavior for the men both on and off the track. ("Always conduct yourself as a gentleman. . . . No honest work is beneath you."[14]) He drew up checklists for drivers and mechanics to follow before every event. ("Be sure you go to the urinal before you start the race."[15]) And he hired a **pit** manager who drilled them in tire changes and fill-ups. At Tacoma, Eddie said his victory "was won in the pit, not on the track."[16]

Eddie's focused driving made him especially competitive on dirt tracks, where rutted curves were a hazard. After winning at Sioux City in 1914, he won there again the next year and a third time the year after that. They called him "King of the Dirt-Track Racers," but in 1916 Eddie had his sights on a loftier title: national champion. He had already won on the board tracks of New York, Omaha, and Tacoma, in addition to the dirt at Sioux City. In September, Eddie needed a win on the bricks in the one-hundred-mile Indianapolis Harvest Classic if he had any hope of catching Johnny Aitken and Dario Resta in championship points.

Eddie came out fast on the two-and-a-half-mile oval, but Aitken's French-built Peugeot was faster. (Resta, already leading in points, chose not to race.) Aitken "was first on the straight-aways," Eddie said, "then I would push him on the curves, and we would come out of it together."[17] For thirty-four laps the two yo-yoed back and forth. Then on the backstretch of the thirty-fifth lap, in the eighty-eighth

that curve," said Eddie.[20] Four different cars narrowly missed ramming him as he slid down the bank toward the inner wall. Eddie stopped in time to see Aitken limping past with only one front wheel still attached! If Eddie had not pressed so hard in the final laps, he might have kept his car in one piece to the finish. Had he known Aitken's car was grievously wounded, he could have—*should have*—held back. He had lost the race by giving it his all, as was his style. Years later, Eddie called it "one of the grandest free-for-alls I ever was in."[21]

The end of the 1916 season was an anticlimax. "I will make every effort to take the lead from Aitken and Resta," Eddie told the papers at the start of November.[22] But the math was against him. He ended the season three weeks later still in third place—but also with a win at the 150-mile Championship Award Sweepstakes in Los Angeles. All he could do was wait until the next year.

In some ways, 1917 looked promising. Eddie had been asked to lead Sunbeam, a strong English-sponsored racing team. On the other hand, dark clouds of war were pushing across the Atlantic, threatening to bring the United States into what was being called a world war. Germany, Austria-Hungary, and Ottoman Turkey—the Central Powers—were fighting a total war against Russia, France, and Great Britain—the **Allies**. Since 1914 the United States had stayed out of the fight, but German U-boats, submarines, were sinking U.S. merchant ships anyway. By 1917, there was no question which side America was on: the Allies'. And if Congress declared war, as seemed likely, there might be no racing season at all.

During a visit to England to consult with his new team, Eddie gazed up at **biplanes** of the Royal Flying Corps zooming back and forth above the River Thames. The sight of these modern wonders planted the seed of an idea in Eddie's head. That seed would sprout into action three months later, when the United States officially entered the war.

DID YOU KNOW?

The Columbus Driving Park, like most early automobile racetracks, was established in the 1800s as a horse-racing oval. In the 1890s, after the Rickenbackers had moved into the little house just down the street, the Driving Park began holding bicycle, motorcycle, and automobile races, too. In 1905, it hosted the world's first twenty-four-hour automobile race. Eddie competed several times on his hometown track, with mostly disappointing results. In 1915 he smashed through the outer fence while his mother, Lizzie, looked on from the stands. The track has been replaced by a park and recreation center, but the neighborhood where Eddie grew up is still known as the Driving Park section of the city.

5

HAT IN THE RING

February 1917 to April 1918

"I have always said that I would rather have a million friends than a million dollars."

—Eddie Rickenbacker[1]

How does a world-class race driver become a fighter pilot in fifteen months? For Rick, as he was now known, it took (once again) hard work and learning by doing. It took having the right friends in the right places and, as he said, no small amount of "**devious**" maneuvering.

THE RIGHT FRIENDS

Rick's idea, born in England, was to recruit American race-car drivers and mechanics to be fighter pilots in the aviation section of the army. As he explained to a reporter after returning to the States, drivers "have a training that our country would need in time of war. We are experts in judging speed and in motor knowledge."[2] Six weeks later, on April 6, Congress declared war, and Rick hurried to Washington to enlist as a

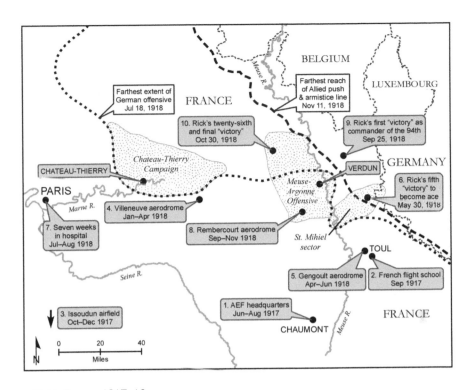

Rick's France, 1917–18
Courtesy of Brian Balsley

fighter pilot. At the same time, he presented his idea for an aero squadron of race-car drivers. Military officials turned him down on both counts. They were looking for college men and Ivy Leaguers to be aviators, not mechanics and sportsmen. They sought men who spoke with polish, not those who sounded as if they just walked in from a workshop floor. Rick had run up against a wall of **class prejudice**. Frustrated, he returned to auto racing.

A week before the big Cincinnati race on Memorial Day (the Indy 500 had been canceled due to the war), Rick received a telephone call from an army official. How would he like to be a driver for General John J. Pershing, commander of the American Expeditionary Forces in

France? Leaders in the AAA had recommended him for the job. Rick jumped at the chance. A couple of weeks later he was "somewhere in France"[3] driving army officials between Paris and AEF headquarters, then between headquarters and various points on the **western front**. It was good work, but Rick was still determined to fly. Again, he bided his time, looking for a chance to make his move.

The opportunity came unexpectedly in Paris when Rick ran into Captain James Miller, a fan from his racing days. Miller had been ordered to establish an American flight-training school at Issoudun and needed a good engineer as his right-hand man. Would Rick be interested? Rick, being Rick, made a counteroffer. "I think an engineering officer for a flying school ought to know how to fly himself," he told Miller.[4] And that was how, "through devious efforts," as Rick put it,[5] he got himself transferred to a flight-training school with the French Air Service in Toul.

LEARNING BY DOING

The French had a curious method for training pilots. After giving careful explanations and demonstrations on the ground, they sent the cadet in the air on his own. The instructor flew behind in a separate aeroplane. Good thing Rick was already an expert at learning by doing.

He and the other cadets started on training planes called "Penguins." They had short little wings like the flightless birds they were named for. The men practiced driving the Penguins on the grass field, pressing the rudder pedals with their feet to turn left or right. They gained just enough speed to practice pulling back the stick, the "elevator," and hopping off the ground a few yards at a time. Rudder and stick: Rick compared the challenge of controlling a plane to "the old trick of patting your head and rubbing your stomach" at the same time.[6]

If his first aeroplane was a Penguin, his next was "a chicken coop." It had "wingspread galore," he said, and "wires all over."[7] Rick struggled to steer it on his first pass over the field. He nearly wrecked it against

A jaunty Sergeant Rickenbacker shows off his uniform and staff car as AEF chauffeur.
Courtesy of the National Museum of the United States Air Force

the **barracks**, but regained control and eventually took off. Landing the craft was trickier. Even after five weeks of training and twenty-five hours in the air—an unusually brief training session in any case—Rick did not quite master the skill of touching down. "I would make a wonderful landing twenty-five feet in the air," he joked.[8]

DEVIOUS MANEUVERS

Rick had become an aviation officer, a first lieutenant, yet his flying days were now officially over. Beginning in October 1917, his job was to oversee the construction of the Issoudun flight-training school. Fields had to be cleared; supplies ordered; **hangars**, barracks, and machine shops assembled. Even before the airfield was completed, American college men began arriving, dressed in sharp uniforms, wearing tall boots and **Sam Browne belts.** Rick resented their ability to fly while he remained grounded. They were cocky and spoiled in his view. Then again, as chief engineer of an airfield still under construction, he had the power to order them to work. He sent them out to haul rocks from the airfields, build roads, and dig **latrines.** "The groaning and moaning . . . were music to my ears," said Rick.[9]

The Ivy Leaguers resented Rick, too. They thought him "tough and uneducated,"[10] "a lemon on an orange tree,"[11] someone who "threw his weight around the wrong way."[12] They made sarcastic remarks behind his back—and sometimes to his face.

Class tensions between the well-bred college men and the street-tough shop mechanic came to a head the day Reed Chambers hot-dogged a landing and narrowly missed crashing into a row of parked planes. Rick raced over on a motorcycle and chewed out the young flier: "Don't you realize we spend our lives here trying to keep these things working?" Chambers didn't give an inch. He even pretended to pull rank. (In fact, he and Rick were both first lieutenants.) Rick, unsure, hesitated, then cut the tension with his famous grin. "Well, all I can say is, I wish I could make that kind of landing." The two had breakfast together, and, just like that, a friendship was born. "He's really a swell

THE KEY TO FLIGHT: ANGLE OF ATTACK

THE ANGLE OF attack is the position at which the wing meets the air. The wing deflects oncoming air downward, which pushes the wing upward. This is called *lift*. The angle of attack needed for lift depends on the speed of the airplane. Faster speed needs less angle of attack. Slower speed needs greater angle of attack. Not enough speed for a given angle of attack leads to a stall. A stall means the airplane is no longer flying but falling. To correct a stall, a pilot must point the nose of the plane down, toward the earth. This allows it to pick up speed, the speed it needs to regain lift.

guy when you get to know him," Chambers told the others.[13] They were unconvinced, but at least Rick had one friend among the aviators.

Meanwhile, Rick was still maneuvering to get himself in the air. Whenever his duties allowed, he stole "a few minutes here and a half hour there"[14] to advance his flying skills. He would slip into the back of the lecture tent to catch the latest flying lesson or sneak an aeroplane out of the hangar to practice flying on his own. Astonishingly, Rick taught himself the **tailspin**, an effective but extremely dangerous maneuver for escaping enemy ambush. Each time, as he spun toward earth, he waited a little longer before tugging the stick, "kicking" the rudder, and pulling out of the spin.

To be a **pursuit pilot**, though, Rick would have to learn to shoot a machine gun while zooming and dipping at one hundred miles an hour. Getting himself released to gunnery school took all the deviousness in Rick's arsenal. He faked an illness and got admitted to the **infirmary**. He hoped to prove that he was expendable, not essential, to the **aerodrome**'s operation. After a week or more of this charade, Major Spatz strode into Rick's sickroom and called his bluff, "I'm onto your little game, Rickenbacker, but, if your heart's set on [flying], you're no good to me here."[15] He gave Rick permission to abandon his engineering post for good.

At gunnery school in January 1918, the cadets stood in rocking boats and fired at moving targets across the lake. It was an awkward task, but the shooting wasn't going to get any easier twelve thousand feet in the air. Rick had poor aim, but with dogged practice—"My shoulder was black and blue from the recoil"[16]—his marksmanship improved.

AND, AGAIN, THE RIGHT FRIENDS

A few weeks later, Rick was in Villeneuve, where all the American aviators in the First Pursuit Group were mobilizing. Their French aeroplanes, Nieuport 28s, were agile and quick . . . but also touchy and unpredictable. More to the point, they had no guns. Even so, the American aviators asked to fly patrols just to show the *Boches*, as the French called the Germans, that they meant business. Their new instructor, Major Raoul Lufbery, agreed to take two new pilots over the lines. He selected Lieutenants Douglas Campbell and Edward Rickenbacker.

In Campbell, Lufbery recognized a top-notch flier. In Rick, he recognized a kindred spirit. Both Luf, as he was known, and Rick were in their late twenties—older than the other pilots. Both were mechanics, not college men. There were several key differences between them, too: Luf was French by birth and American by choice. He had already flown two years on the western front as a member of the **Lafayette Escadrille**. He had already mastered the art of flying and the tactics of aerial combat. Like Lee Frayer before him, Luf became Rick's mentor. "Everything I learned, I learned from Lufbery," Rick would say.[17]

The morning of March 28, 1918, dawned fair and cool, but at fifteen thousand feet, the air would be near zero degrees Fahrenheit in an open-cockpit aeroplane. So Luf, Campbell, and Rick wore fur-lined leather suits and helmets. Glass goggles protected their eyes but would quickly become spattered with **castor oil** spewed from the spinning cylinders of the rotary engine.

It was cold at fifteen thousand feet. Rick and the other pilots wore fur-lined suits.
Courtesy of Auburn University Libraries Special Collections and Archives

Rick put his "hat in the ring" along with the other officers of the 94th Aero Squadron.
Courtesy of Auburn University Libraries Special Collections and Archives

Luf instructed Rick and Campbell to scan the skies—right, left, up, down—for enemy planes. "Vision of the air," he called it.[18] He demonstrated a corkscrew maneuver, using light touches of rudder and stick to weave through the air. It made them a harder target for enemy guns. All the corkscrewing of the plane and swiveling of the head made Rick nauseated. Swallowing gulps of sprayed castor oil made him truly sick. Flight mechanics cleaned up the vomit in his cockpit after he returned to the airfield.

In the following days, other pilots flew patrols over the lines, and Rick learned to overcome the nausea. Then, in early April, their machine guns arrived and were mounted on the Nieuport 28s. The men were divided into squadrons of twenty men each. Each aero squadron chose an insignia to paint on its planes. The 95th chose a kicking mule: stubborn and strong. Rick's squadron, the 94th, selected an upside-down stovepipe hat with stars and stripes, like Uncle Sam tipping his hat, inside a surrounding circle. One member of the group remarked, "Well, I guess our hat is in the ring now!"[19]

And so it was, on April 14, 1918, from Gengoult aerodrome outside Toul, the Hat-in-the-Ring Squadron entered the Great War for real in the skies over the western front.

DID YOU KNOW?

When the first Indianapolis 500 was run in 1911, Memorial Day was also known as Decoration Day, a time to decorate the graves of Civil War dead with flowers. Towns chose their own spring date to celebrate it, before May 30, eventually, became accepted around the country. As the century progressed, and Americans fought and died in more wars, beginning with World War I, the name Decoration Day gradually dropped out of use. Today Memorial Day falls on the last Monday of May, and the Indianapolis 500 is run on the Sunday before that.

ACE OF ACES

April 1918 to November 1918

"If you have a gimper with you, you know he won't make a mistake in judgment or lose his nerve at the critical time."

—Eddie Rickenbacker[1]

Rick's first patrol from Toul did not go well. Flying into a thick mist, Captain Peterson chose to turn back after takeoff. Rick misread the commander's wing-wagging signal and continued the patrol with his buddy Reed Chambers. Back and forth the novices flew across the Saint-Mihiel **sector**. They saw no enemy planes but did encounter bursts of "Archie," German **antiaircraft**, fire. Turning toward home after ninety minutes in the air, Rick was alarmed to see how thick the cloud cover had become. Somehow, he and Chambers had to find their airfield before fuel ran out.

Dipping below the clouds, Rick recognized a railroad track and followed it back to the aerodrome. But Chambers was nowhere to be seen. Captain Peterson met Rick on the ground and called him a "bloody fool" for flying off in bad weather. Rick was distraught. "I was posi-

Rick in his Nieuport 28
Courtesy of the National Museum of the United States Air Force

tive the telephone would ring within a few minutes to inform us that Chambers had crashed and killed himself in the fog."[2]

Instead, it rang to say that two enemy fighter planes were sighted overhead. Rick and Chambers had unintentionally drawn them across the line. Two other pilots from the 94th, Campbell and Alan Winslow, ran to their Nieuports. Mechanics yanked down the propellers—*Contact!*—and the engines roared to life. Within minutes, Campbell and Winslow had brought down the first enemy planes of the war for the Americans, and the residents of Toul took to the streets to celebrate their new heroes. "*Vivent les Américains!*" they cheered,[3] but Rick could not share in the joy. He was sickened by the thought that he might have lost a friend. To his relief, Chambers was driven into camp a few hours later after surviving a **forced landing.**

WHY WERE ANTIAIRCRAFT SHELLS CALLED "ARCHIES"?

MISHAPS AND CRACK-UPS were all part of the game when learning to fly for the Royal Flying Corps. But the British cadets noticed an unusually high amount of crashes into the local "sewer farm," where nutrient-rich waste water was stored for crop irrigation.[4] Tongue in cheek, they gave the swamp a nickname, Archibald, or Archie. After a crash in the sewage farm they might say: *I had a run-in with Archie this morning.*

Later, when they went over **the Channel** to fly actual combat patrols, British pilots wondered if German antiaircraft shells might have the same mysterious attraction as the sewage farm. They called them "Archies" as a kind of inside joke. American pilots adopted the same slang, even if they never knew where the name came from.

More frustrations—and some anguish—awaited Rick over the next several weeks. He made more mistakes, any one of which might have ended his flying career. Several times, he came within a whisker of shooting down a plane that turned out to be friendly, either American or French. He thought he was going to crash the time his wing's fabric tore off the frame. Worst of all, on May 19, his beloved Luf was killed in combat.

But fate smiled on Rick, too, as it always had in the past. He made his first "victory," downing an enemy plane, on April 29. A week later, he was made a flight commander, in charge of six other pilots in the squadron. By June, he had shot down five enemy planes, qualifying him to be an ace. He was the second pilot in the squadron to earn the title and, with it, the privilege of flying over enemy lines by himself in voluntary patrols.

Rick chose to fly his patrols with a **wingman**, Walter Smythe, a young lieutenant he had taken a liking to. Together, on June 4, Rick and Smythe encountered a German observation plane flying over French

Rick's closest brush with disaster happened when the fabric on his
Nieuport's wing tore off during a dive. Here he poses with the dam-
aged wing.
Courtesy of Auburn University Libraries Special Collections and Archives

All were eager to be tested, but Rick would not go with them. He had a raging fever and spent a week in the hospital. Five days after release, he was sent back to the hospital with a painful earache. Even after surgery, the pain continued. Rick returned to Paris for a second operation, which, this time, did the trick. But he still missed another three weeks for recovery. In fact, Rick missed seven weeks during the entire two-month Chateau-Thierry campaign—a period in which thirty-one American fliers were either killed, wounded, or captured (including Smythe, killed while his mentor lay bedridden in Paris).

What seemed at the time like the worst bad luck turned out, in retrospect, to be a kind of blessing. The forced confinement allowed Rick valuable time to reflect on his mistakes. "Most of one's troubles in this world come from something wrong inside oneself," he reflected.[8] So Rick looked inside himself and found a want of self-discipline. When he got back in the air—*if* he got back in the air—he vowed to show restraint. He would avoid combats that had less than a fifty-fifty chance of success. "Cool, calculating, and careful" would be his watchwords.[9]

The weeks Rick missed were not good ones for the Hat-in-the-Ring Squadron either. Its members received new, more powerful Spad XIIIs, yet the planes experienced frequent engine problems that too often left the squadron on the ground, awaiting repairs. When they did get in the air, the results were discouraging. More Hat-in-the-Ring Spads were brought down that summer (five) than German Fokkers they shot down (two).[10]

So the squadron's leader, Captain Marr, was relieved of command on September 24, just before the big Meuse-Argonne offensive. (Now it was the Allies' turn to make a big push toward Germany.) In his place, Major Hartney named the once-hated engineer of Issoudun, Lieutenant Rickenbacker. He selected Rick over three higher-ranked captains and college men because he had a hunch Rick was the man for the job.

Rick proved him right from the very first day. He gathered his pilots and mechanics in a hangar at Rembercourt aerodrome and spoke to them firmly about the need to step up their game. Their job was to bring down enemy planes, not to worry about army rules and regulations. He "didn't want anybody wasting time saluting somebody else."[11] To mechanics, he said he was one of them and understood the importance of their role. He gave them his full support, and they gave the squadron theirs in return. In short, Rick was turning the 94th Aero Squadron "back into a team."[12]

The next morning Rick put his words into action by taking a solo patrol at dawn. Sneaking up on a formation of five enemy planes, he downed two of them. Hearing the news, the men of the Hat-in-the-Ring understood their commander was a "gimper": a leader who would never ask them to do something he wouldn't first do himself, a pilot who would not shrink from danger or lose his nerve under pressure. Commander Eddie Rickenbacker was in "the game"[13] to win, and the men of the 94th knew it.

Over the next six weeks, the last of the war, the Hat-in-the-Ring Squadron rose to Rick's high expectations. Its members downed forty-four enemy planes and lost only five of their own. Rick accounted for eighteen of those victories himself, often against enemy formations that outnumbered him by two- or even four-to-one. Had Rick forgotten his pledge to be more cautious? No. Rick remained a bold fighter—one who flew more patrols than anyone else in the squadron—but also one aware at all times of what he could and could not do. "I knew my limitations," he said.[14]

The announcement of the armistice to end the war came over the telephone on the night of November 10, 1918. A flood of joyous relief swept over the American airmen, and Rick joined in the frenzy. But in the morning, he awoke in a serious frame of mind. He wanted to take his trusty Spad XIII on one last solo patrol. He wanted to be aloft when the war officially ended on the eleventh hour of the eleventh day of the eleventh month.

At the appointed hour, Rick looked down on the shell-pocked waste known as No Man's Land. He watched thousands of Germans and Americans leap from their trenches. He saw them throw down their guns, toss their helmets in the air, and run together into a swirling mass of gray and brown uniforms. Men who, minutes before, had been

Rickenbacker was promoted to captain in late October, just before the end of the war. This photograph shows him after the war, with captain's stripes on his shoulders and Distinguished Service Cross, Légion d'honneur, and Croix de guerre medals on his chest.
Courtesy of Auburn University Libraries Special Collections and Archives

pointing guns at each other were now dancing and hugging like children.[15] They had survived the Great War.

And so had the recently promoted *Captain* Rickenbacker. But what were he and his men to do now that "the zest and excitement of fighting airplanes" had ended?[16]

A German balloon company sends its *Drachen* aloft.
Courtesy of Creative Commons

DID YOU KNOW?

Observation balloons were the most important targets of
pursuit pilots on the western front. (Rick shot down four.)
They were "the eyes of the artillery," helping the big guns on
each side adjust their aim.[17] The French thought these giant
gas bags looked like sausages, *sauçisses*. The Germans called
them *Drachen,* dragons. Shooting them down was much
harder than it appeared. Even Rick's best-planned multi-
plane attacks ended as often as not in failure. Lieutenant
Frank Luke was America's greatest balloon buster. Luke shot
down fourteen balloons in ten days of patrols and became
America's Ace of Aces for thirteen days—until his reckless-
ness ultimately got him killed.

GROUNDED

February 1919 to December 1934

"Successes don't just happen.... They come from
foresight and planning."

—Eddie Rickenbacker[1]

N OW WHAT?

Ever since his father's death, Rickenbacker's life had been driven in the highest gear. Sure, there had been pit stops (the months selling Firestone-Columbuses in Omaha) and breakdowns (the wall of military prejudice that kept him from flying), but this was different. Half a lifetime stretched before him. Did he have the patience to work up the ladder all over again? Could he bear taking orders rather than giving them? These were big questions facing Rickenbacker when he stepped off the RMS *Adriatic* onto American soil on February 1, 1919.

But he didn't have to answer them just yet. Eddie Rickenbacker was a war hero, and he was treated to a hero's welcome. At a banquet in the Waldorf-Astoria Hotel, six hundred friends and admirers "cheered him and toasted him and shouted and sang to him."[2] In Columbus, a "barrage of kisses" greeted him as he stepped from the train.[3] Los

Rickenbacker was a national hero, but there was no one he wanted to impress more than his mother.
Courtesy of Auburn University Libraries Special Collections and Archives

Angeles held a three-day celebration in his honor, highlighted by a citywide parade. Rickenbacker rode in an automobile fitted with wings, covered with colorful flowers. "It was stunningly beautiful," said the Ace of Aces, "but I felt like an idiot riding in it for three hours."[4]

Between the New York banquet and the Los Angeles parade, Rickenbacker signed a book deal worth more than twenty-five thousand dollars and a speaking tour contract worth ten thousand dollars. The

I'M GLAD TO BE BACK IN THE U.S.A.

MY SENTIMENTS

Oh, I'm glad to be back in the U. S. A.
It surely is the place for me;
I helped Uncle Sam and the Allies
In their fight across the sea;
I've been in London town and thot it fine,
I've been in Gay Paree and across the Rhine
Now I'm glad to be back with the home folks,
The U. S. A's. the place for mine.

Enterprising Americans would do anything to capitalize on Rickenbacker's fame,
even using his picture to help sell a new song.
Courtesy of Hocking County Historical and Genealogical Society and Museum

WHAT'S IN A NAME?

WHEN RICKENBACKER FIRST started seeing his name in print, back in his racing days, he thought it "looked a little plain."[5] So he decided to give himself what his parents hadn't: a middle name. After experimenting with different initials, writing them over and over, he liked the way "V" looked and how he could write it in script between "E" and "R" without stopping.[6] He tried "Victor" for a while but ultimately settled on the name of a friend from childhood—the brother of Blanche Calhoun, the girl in Sunday school he used to paint pictures for. That's how the Ace of Aces became Edward *Vernon* Rickenbacker—though most Americans called him, simply, Captain Eddie.

sum was more than the winner's prize money at the Indianapolis 500 that year. Clothing, chewing gum, and cigarette companies asked him to endorse their products at five thousand dollars a pop. A Hollywood producer offered him one hundred thousand dollars to star in a movie. Rickenbacker turned these down. He needed the money, but he didn't want to cheapen his image. "It would just utterly destroy much of the hero worship among the kids," he said.[7]

When the **ballyhoo** quieted down, Rickenbacker was still without a regular income. Would he get a job in automobiles or aviation? "There is no comparison between the auto and the air," Rickenbacker told reporters. "I am through with the automobile, and I stand ready to place my skill and talents in flying."[8] He may have "stood ready" for a career in aviation, but aviation—in the United States in 1919—wasn't ready for him. There were few airfields and exactly zero airlines. Regular airmail would not arrive for five years. Regular passenger service wouldn't develop for another five years after that.

Rickenbacker did his part to try to hurry matters along. In 1920, he and two other men flew a trio of German Junkers planes across the

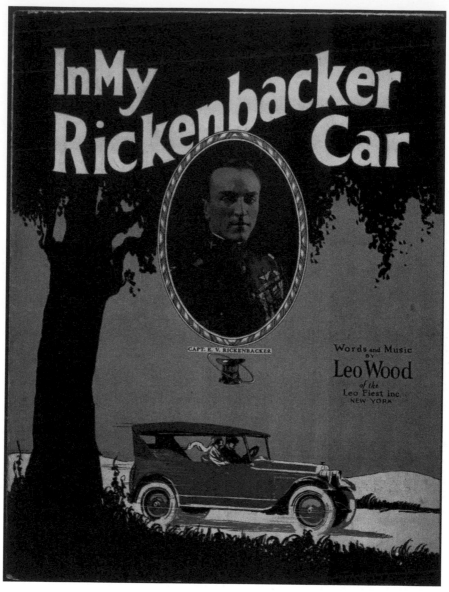

In 1923, Rickenbacker received free publicity for his car when Leo Wood composed a song about it. Among the lyrics' rhymes: "She won't jar your vacation / For there's no vibration," and "Merrily I roll along in my cracker jacker Rickenbacker."[9]
Courtesy of the Columbus Metropolitan Library Image Collections

country to show how easily it could be done. With two crack-ups (one into the side of a house!), two near misses, and two forced landings, they proved precisely the reverse: it wasn't easy at all. On another trip, mechanical problems forced four emergency landings: in a wheat field, a cornfield, a cotton field, and beside an outdoor high school graduation. He gave up in Iowa after rolling into the ditch on takeoff. Two more **transcontinental** trips brought four accidents, three close calls, two forced landings, and—improbably—one transcontinental speed record, fifty-eight hours.[10]

Aviation was still very much in development.

So Rickenbacker went back to automobiles. More precisely, to one automobile in particular: the Rickenbacker, "A Car Worthy of Its Name." He found an investor with money to back his project. Then he hired an engineer and a production man to design and build his car. It took two years of work and one hundred thousand miles of test driving before Rickenbacker was satisfied. The first Rickenbacker automobile went on sale in early 1922.

Rickenbacker was in business but also, for the first time, in love. Adelaide Frost Durant had left a troubled marriage to an unruly race-car driver and fell into Rickenbacker's arms in her distress. Rickenbacker welcomed her attentions and kept finding excuses to get to New York to visit her. Before the year was out, the two were married and on a six-week honeymoon to Europe. They set up house in Detroit, and Rickenbacker got back to work selling his car.

It wasn't a hard sell—at first. No other mid-priced car had so smooth a ride. No other provided the security of four-wheel brakes. Unfortunately, high quality and a moderate price made for a slim **profit**. In the competitive **market** of the mid-1920s, the Rickenbacker Motor Company began losing money. Before long it went out of business. "We were broke flatter than a pancake," Rickenbacker said.[11]

The man who had succeeded in everything he set his mind to had failed. "It was too good a car," Rickenbacker grumbled.[12] Maybe so, but it was also true that Rickenbacker had not set his *whole* mind to selling

Eddie on his honeymoon with Adelaide (and pigeons) in St. Mark's Square, Venice, Italy.
Courtesy of Auburn University Libraries Special Collections and Archives

his car. A part of him had kept an eye on and a hand in aviation. On the side, Rickenbacker had been designing a low-cost airplane engine (which never caught on) and had also teamed up with his Hat-in-the-Ring buddy Reed Chambers to establish an airline in Florida.

On April 1, 1926, as Rickenbacker Motors was sinking, Florida Airways carried its first load of airmail from Miami to Jacksonville. On June 1, it carried its first passenger. But seven months, thirteen thousand pounds of mail, and 930 passengers later, the airline went out of business, too. "We were just too far ahead of the game," Rickenbacker grumbled again.[13] The Ace of Aces had suffered two business failures in less than a year. Worse, he owed the bank $250,000. He could have escaped responsibility for the debts in **bankruptcy** court, but that was not Rickenbacker's way. "I owed the money, and I would pay it back if I had to work like a dog to do it," he said.[14]

How does a man without a job pay back a quarter of a million dollars? Surely not by borrowing even more money. Yet that is exactly what Rickenbacker did. Capitalizing on his good name (one of the best known in the country) and his good **credit** (as demonstrated by his not declaring personal bankruptcy), he was able to get a loan for seven hundred thousand dollars to buy the Indianapolis Motor Speedway. It didn't hurt that Adelaide had been the favored daughter-in-law of Billy Durant, founder of General Motors. To the marriage, she brought both money and a connection to one of the most important companies in the automotive world. Before the year was out, Rickenbacker was working full time for GM, selling Cadillacs and La Salles, in addition to managing the Indianapolis Motor Speedway. Only in May, when the Indianapolis 500 was held, did the Speedway require his full attention.

Because the couple was unable to have children of their own, Eddie and Adelaide adopted two sons, David in 1925 and William in 1928. Their family was growing, and, with it, Rickenbacker's sense of responsibility. As he always had in the past, Rickenbacker hustled to get ahead. He studied the emerging field of commercial aviation, he listened to experts, and he learned. By making shrewd investments and working

The Ace of Aces as father, early 1930s, with his sons, Dave and Bill (*both with blond hair, on the left*)
Courtesy of Auburn University Libraries Special Collections and Archives

eighteen-hour days, he was able to earn enough to pay back his debts—and gain the experience he needed to reach the top of the airline management field.

In December 1934, after having relocated his family to greater New York City and having worked four different aviation jobs, Rickenbacker was selected to be general manager of an airline owned and operated by General Motors: Eastern Air Lines. His decade-and-a-half scramble up the ladder had ended in success. Captain Eddie was back in command and determined to turn Eastern into a winning team, just as he had the Hat-in-the-Ring Squadron sixteen years before. As it happened, one more struggle awaited before he would be fully at the controls.

DID YOU KNOW?

In 1910 more than 250 automobile companies were making motorcars in the United States. By 1930 there were fewer than 40. Ford dominated the market in the 1910s with its inexpensive, durable Model T. By the end of the decade, more than half of all cars on the road were Tin Lizzies, as the Model T was affectionately called. General Motors surpassed Ford in the 1920s by selling many different makes and models. "A car for every purse and purpose," the new president, Alfred Sloan, liked to say.[15] Mid-decade, Walter Chrysler introduced a stylish and powerful new car at an affordable price: the Chrysler Six. It competed in the same mid-priced market as the Rickenbacker (and it won). By the end of the decade, people were talking about the Big Three automobile makers: Chrysler, GM, and Ford.

8

AT THE CONTROLS

January 1935 to January 1942

"I am in the greatest business in the world, as well as working for the greatest company in the world."
—Eddie Rickenbacker[1]

THE YEAR 1935 was a good one to take command of an airline. In their earliest years, airlines had been glorified mail carriers. They tried to lure passengers into the air, but the fear of leaving the ground (never mind the expense) was too great for most travelers. Those who overcame their anxiety had to deal with unexpected discomforts. Airline passengers could barely talk over the roar of the engines or stay in their seats from all the bumping and rocking. Stale air in the cabin smelled, as often as not, of vomit mixed with disinfectant.[2]

But in 1935, a new and improved passenger plane had just come on line. It flew higher, and therefore faster and smoother, than earlier models. Rickenbacker purchased ten DC-2s right away and added even more of the sleeker, larger DC-3s the next year. With its fleet of shiny, new planes Eastern Air Lines began calling itself "the Great Silver Fleet."[3]

Captain Eddie was a hands-on **executive**, a people person. He logged thousands of miles visiting Eastern's destination cities, mostly

A DC-3 in the Great Silver Fleet, 1939
Courtesy of Creative Commons

in the southeastern United States. At each airport, he would find ways to "pitch in and help."[4] He carried baggage and checked people in, changed tires, and made reservations for stranded passengers. No one knew all sides of the company better than the man at the top.

Rickenbacker still knew how to work publicity to his advantage. Eastern got in the newspapers for setting records (*Eastern Air Line Flies 22 Persons, Non-Stop, for 1,231 Miles*), daring exploits (*Crack Eastern Air Lines' Pilot Will Fly South to Aid Antarctic Explorer*), and plain old human-interest stories (*Basketball Star Misses Bus, Eastern Plane Whisks Boy to Capital for Game*).[5]

As ever, Rickenbacker was a problem solver. He maximized planes' time in the air and minimized their time on the ground. As a result, for the first time in its history, Eastern Air Lines actually *earned* money. It was the first time any American passenger airline had made a profit.

With business picking up, it might seem an odd time for General Motors to get out of the aviation business. But that is exactly what GM was planning to do. They had a buyer lined up willing to pay three million dollars for their profitable airline. Rickenbacker heard the rumors and panicked. He feared he would lose his dream job under the new ownership. He went back to the banks and convinced them to loan him three and a *half* million dollars to buy Eastern outright. (Later he would sell stock, part ownership in the company, to raise money.)

On April 19, 1938, Eddie Rickenbacker, former Ace of Aces and King of the Dirt-Track Racers, added a new title to his name: president and chief executive officer of Eastern Air Lines. On the occasion, Rickenbacker wrote down a set of rules for himself, much as he had done for the drivers and mechanics on his race team twenty-two years earlier. "My Constitution," he called it. In it, he promised to "plan my work, work my plan" and "sell, sell, sell Eastern Air Lines." He declared that he was working "in the greatest business in the world" and "for the greatest company in the world."[6]

Eastern Air Lines was now Rickenbacker's, and his alone. So it's not surprising the company took on the character of the man at the top. That man was both a stern taskmaster *and* a kindly father-figure, a sharp-tongued critic *and* a supportive ally, a tight-fisted Scrooge *and* a generous patron. No manager at Eastern was permitted to spend more than fifty dollars without the Captain's specific approval. Yet Rickenbacker never blinked about writing larger checks for employees in a crisis. He sent paychecks to any man or woman out of work for illness—and often paid their hospital bills, too.[7]

Most of all, Rickenbacker was still a gimper. No one worked harder or longer: every hour of most days, every day of most weeks. Dave and Bill rarely saw their father; the work of parenting fell mostly to their mother, Adelaide. In 1939, when Dave was thirteen and Bill just eleven, the boys were sent away to boarding school. Rickenbacker's relationships with his children were conducted mostly by letter.

Rickenbacker was so busy in these years that he sometimes had to be in two places at once. Such was the case on February 26, 1941. Airline boosters in Birmingham, Alabama, begged him to speak at a luncheon on a day he was supposed to be in Miami. He had put these men off

Rickenbacker was still the owner of the Indianapolis Motor Speedway and the director of the Indianapolis 500 every May. Here he is with Dave (*left*) and Bill before the big race, about 1940.
Courtesy of Auburn University Libraries Special Collections and Archives

before. He could not do it again. Reluctantly, Rickenbacker changed his plans and went to Alabama.

But first he had to fly through Atlanta.

Captain Eddie was working on his speech in the Sky Lounge, just behind the cockpit, when the young Eastern Air Lines' pilot came back with a concern. Atlanta was reporting bad weather. Should he turn the plane around, just to be safe? Rickenbacker understood what the young pilot was asking. He wanted the boss to make the tough call. But Rickenbacker had a policy never to interfere with his pilots. "Don't let me worry you," he told the pilot. "Don't let my being on board affect your decision in any way. Use your judgment. That's your job."[8] The pilot returned to the cockpit, the full weight of the decision on his shoulders.

He chose to fly on to Atlanta's Candler Field, where the ceiling, cloud cover, had dropped to less than three hundred feet. As he banked in his approach, the left wing brushed the tops of the trees. Instinctively, he corrected—*over*corrected—and hit the trees with the right wing. But not before Rickenbacker dove down the aisle toward the rear of the plane, where he knew he would be safer in the coming crash.

He didn't get far before the plane cartwheeled through the pine trees, plunged nose first into the ground, and, as Rickenbacker explained later, corkscrewed "like when a kid takes a paper bag and twists it to hold the air in."[9] Rickenbacker landed on the roof of the upside-down plane, pinned by crushed metal, in utter darkness. Covered in blood and gasoline, he somehow had the strength to shout, "For God's sake, *don't light a match!*"[10] No one did, and the eight survivors of seventeen on board spent a long, painful night, groaning, until a search party found them in the woods at dawn.

Rickenbacker was the worst injured of the eight. His whole left side was mangled: hip smashed, elbow shattered, knee splintered, hand bent, ribs cracked, nerves crushed, eyeball wrenched from its socket and dangling on his cheek. "He's more dead than alive," an attendant muttered when Rickenbacker finally reached the hospital.[11] But the Captain surprised them all. He got better . . . before he got worse again. Death lingered over his hospital bed. "I felt myself pushing my toes into the pearly gates," he said, and it was "the sweetest, tenderest . . . sensation I have ever experienced."[12] Another man might have given in to the sweetness. Not Rickenbacker. Through a haze of **delirium**, he heard a voice come over the radio. *It's confirmed that Eddie Rickenbacker is dying and is not expected to live out the hour.* Rickenbacker hurled a pitcher of water at the radio and fought for life all the harder. "I'm not dead," he shouted, "and I'm not going to die."[13]

Rickenbacker was right, but recovery was long in coming, involved complicated surgeries, and was never complete. He would wear a special shoe and walk with a slight limp for the rest of his life. (On the other hand, his eyeball was returned to its socket, and his vision re-

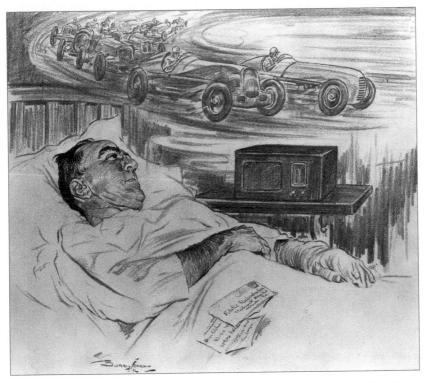

Eddie said he received seven thousand telegrams and eighteen thousand total "communications" from well-wishers during his four-month stay in the Atlanta hospital.[14] Here an artist imagines him reading letters, listening to the radio, and dreaming of his glory days on the racetrack.
Courtesy of Auburn University Libraries Special Collections and Archives

mained normal.) After four months in the hospital, Rickenbacker returned to New York to lead his airline, only at a slower pace. As had happened before—the Pennsylvania Railroad injury, the ear infection in France—enforced rest gave him the opportunity to think. On a beach in southern Florida in the winter of 1942, Rickenbacker realized he must have been "permitted to continue living for some good purpose."[15] That purpose, surely, had something to do with the second world-encompassing war the United States was just entering.

Ace Drummond movie poster, 1936
Courtesy Wikimedia Commons

DID YOU KNOW?

Rickenbacker created a comic strip hero in the 1930s called Ace Drummond. The Sunday strip followed the adventures of a young flying ace defeating evil and fighting for good. Clayton Knight, another WWI aviator, teamed up with Rickenbacker as the strip's illustrator. The two produced a weekly nonfiction feature, too, called *Hall of Fame of the Air*. Each week they focused on the accomplishments of a different aviation pioneer from around the world. The *Ace Drummond* strip appeared in 130 newspapers. In 1936, it was adapted into a movie serial that ran for thirteen episodes.

9

MAYDAY

December 1941 to August 1945

"I'll fight like a wildcat until they nail the lid of my pine box down on me."
—Eddie Rickenbacker[1]

T HE WORLD was at war for the second time in a generation. Rickenbacker had anticipated the conflict as far back as 1922, when on his honeymoon with Adelaide. In Berlin, he saw a "gleam in the eye of a group of German former fighter pilots" they visited.[2] One of them had bragged, "It is by air power that we are going to recapture the German empire," as if the war had not ended just four years earlier. A second trip to Europe in 1935 revealed how far the Germans had advanced in their preparations. Rickenbacker was impressed by their well-run training bases and humming factories—but a little put off by their boasting. He understood just how far the United States lagged behind. So, he returned to the States and shared his concern. No one listened to him. He wrote up a plan for peacetime preparedness. No one acted on it.

Rickenbacker wanted his country to *prepare* for war because he did not want it to *go* to war, which he called "scientific murder,"[3] "an atrocious evil,"[4] and "a cold heartless business of killing men and

Rickenbacker took two more trips to Europe with his family in 1938 and 1939. Here he is on the steamer, 1938, with (*left to right*) Bill, Adelaide, and Dave. Courtesy of Auburn University Libraries Special Collections and Archives

destroying property."[5] America's boys and girls should be free to enjoy marbles, baseball, and model airplanes, he said, not be "regimented into uniforms" and taught to shoulder guns.[6] Military strength for Rickenbacker was primarily defensive: to keep enemies from getting any ideas about attacking.

But events moved ahead quickly and so did Rickenbacker's thinking. On the strength of its air force, Germany was taking control of Europe. Poland, Norway, Netherlands, Belgium, and France had fallen under German control. Now Britain was under heavy bombardment. "The sooner we crush Hitler the better," Rickenbacker told a reporter upon his release from the Atlanta hospital.[7]

Six months later, on December 7, 1941, the Japanese Navy Air Service attacked the U.S. naval base at Pearl Harbor, Hawaii. The United States was at war again, and Rickenbacker was called to serve his country . . . again. Over the next two years, he went on three "tours of inspection"[8] for the U.S. Army Air Forces, both in the United States and abroad.

On the first tour, he was asked to boost **morale** among pilots frustrated by a lack of equipment and flying time. "Go out and talk to these boys," Lieutenant General Henry "Hap" Arnold, chief of the U.S. Army Air Forces, told him. "Inspire them, put some fire in them."[9] Fifteen thousand miles of travel and pep talks at forty-one bases in thirty-one days was a lot to ask of a man whose body still pained him every day. But the AAF chief was pleased with Rickenbacker's results. "Your talks were straight to the point and were a source of greatest inspiration to our young pilots," Arnold said.[10]

On the second tour, Rickenbacker was asked to determine the readiness of Army Air Force units stationed in the United Kingdom and evaluate the strength of their planes. A third tour took him halfway around the world and back, covering fifty-five thousand miles and a dozen countries. Wherever he went, he talked, he listened, and he observed. Then he wrote up lengthy reports for his superiors. Wherever he saw weaknesses, he made detailed suggestions for improvement. But in public he always defended the AAF planes against criticism. "Remember," he told a radio audience, "no one plane can perform

A B-17 "Flying Fortress," like the one Rickenbacker and his crew flew on the Pacific mission
Courtesy Wikimedia Commons

every type of mission. . . . You've got to do one job or the other—or compromise."[11]

As president and chairman of Eastern Air Lines, Rickenbacker also donated more than half of his company's planes and crews to the Air Transport Command, the unit that carried people and supplies for the armed forces. He convinced other airline presidents to do the same. "This is the time when you're going to have to think about your country first and your airline second," he told them.[12] As owner of the Indianapolis Motor Speedway, he shut down the track so race drivers and mechanics could join one of the armed services, just as he had done in the previous war.

Between the United Kingdom mission and the world mission, Rickenbacker went on a Pacific mission to deliver a top-secret message

INTERNATIONAL DISTRESS CALLS: SOS AND MAYDAY

MAYDAY HAS BEEN an international **distress call** since 1923. It comes from the French phrase, *m'aidez* (pronounced "med-*day*"), for "help me." SOS has been in use for Morse code since 1908. The letters in Morse—dot-dot-dot, dash-dash-dash, dot-dot-dot—were chosen because they are easily tapped out and easily recognized. Only later was the phrase "Save Our Ship" added as a possible meaning. The radio operator on Rickenbacker's B-17 sent a Morse SOS, not a spoken Mayday.

from secretary of war Henry Stimson to General Douglas MacArthur, supreme commander of Allied Forces in the Southwest Pacific Area. Rickenbacker, escorted by a crew of seven men, was to fly from Hawaii to Australia, 4,700 miles away. Along the way, they had to find the refueling point, Canton Island, the first stop in their hop, skip, and jump across the Pacific.

But Canton was a tiny speck amid the vast blue, and they missed it. Unable to get a bearing from the island's poorly equipped radio station and running out of fuel, they prepared to make a watery emergency landing. Captain William Cherry Jr. set the plane down perfectly between the crests of two waves. Even so, two of the eight men were injured in the abrupt stop.

Within minutes, all eight sat cramped in three small life rafts, buffeted by eight-foot waves and menaced by circling sharks. They took stock of their possessions: a rope, a first-aid kit, two bailing buckets, two knives, two fishhooks and a line, a compass, a map of the Pacific, a Bible, and four oranges. In their rush to evacuate the sinking plane, however, the men had forgotten to bring the emergency stores of food and water. Four measly oranges were all they had to share between eight people. No one knew how long the supplies might have to last. Not one of them could have guessed it would be more than three weeks.

Sporadic rainstorms saved them from **dehydration**. During **squalls**, the men captured fresh water in bailing buckets and pouches in their life vests, enough to ration a tablespoon or two most days.

Good luck (the men believed it was God's grace) provided them barely enough calories to survive. At the end of the first week, as the strictly rationed oranges ran out, a wayward seabird landed atop Rickenbacker's floppy hat. At once, seven pairs of "hungry, famished, almost insane eyes" implored him to grab it.[13] Rickenbacker lifted his hand slowly and, instead of making a last-instant grab, merely closed his fingers around the tern's legs, pulled it down, wrung its neck, and yanked out its feathers. The scrawny bird, divided eight ways and gobbled down raw, gave the men hardly a mouthful. Yet the intestines, baited to the fishhooks, yielded two mackerel pulled from the sea. During the next two weeks, a couple of leaping fish that landed in the boat and a few handfuls of "fingerling" minnows scooped from the sea supplied their only other nourishment.

Rickenbacker's willpower kept the group from giving up when hope gave way to despair in the third week. The youngest member of the group, Staff Sergeant Alex Kazmarzcyk, died on day thirteen. Already weakened by a recent appendix operation, he had given in to the temptation to drink seawater, which speeds up dehydration. Some of the others began to dream of following Sergeant Alex into the world beyond suffering. That's when Rickenbacker took over. If anyone spoke of giving up, he would jump on the man with all the ferocity of a wildcat, letting loose a "masterpiece" of cussing, as the copilot, Lieutenant Whittaker, put it. "Why you blanketty blank blank quitter!" he would rail.[14] The men grew to hate him for his scolding—which was exactly what he wanted. "If [a man] could snarl back at me," Rickenbacker explained, "he could snarl back at death."[15]

The seven, gaunt and blistered, survived long enough to be spotted after twenty-three days at sea. Lieutenant William Eadie set down his

Kingfisher pontoon plane and called, "Well, Captain Rickenbacker, here we are!"[16] His grin must have been as wide as the Pacific itself. Eadie and his radioman pulled Rickenbacker and the others up on the plane's wing and strapped them down. The survivors were overcome with gratitude. "God bless the Navy!" Rickenbacker rasped.[17]

Three weeks later, after putting on twenty of the fifty-four pounds he had lost, Rickenbacker insisted on completing his mission to General MacArthur. Along the way, he met worn, exhausted soldiers coming out of the battle zone. He learned of the hellish conditions in which they fought in the jungles of Guadalcanal. This experience, coming on the heels of his three-week ordeal, changed Rickenbacker and his approach to the war. No more would he defend a military system that was anything less than meticulous, exacting, in its preparations. No more would he temper his words or worry if he "stepped on tender toes."[18] He criticized the nation's war effort publicly and did step on toes—even those of President Franklin Roosevelt. To everyday Americans he scolded, "You . . . should be grateful for the privilege of offering everything you know how. . . . For none of us are doing so much that we cannot do more."[19] In speeches and radio broadcasts, Rickenbacker was selling his philosophy of life to an entire nation.

Some wondered if Rickenbacker was positioning himself to make a run for president. Some wished he would put his "hat in the ring" for the presidency. But Rickenbacker insisted he wanted to remain a private citizen, free to speak his mind however he saw fit. Besides, as he told one supporter, "You know I couldn't possibly win. I'm too controversial."[20]

The war ended in victory, with American freedom secured. Rickenbacker had played his part, but he was not the unifying hero he had been after the last war. He was a polarizing figure now—loved by some, despised by others (though there were more of the first than of the second). Rickenbacker would embrace his role as a teller of unpleasant truths, even as he returned full-time to building his airline in the final phase of his career.

Rickenbacker continuing his Pacific mission, looking thinner but all smiles.
Courtesy of Auburn University Libraries Special Collections and Archives

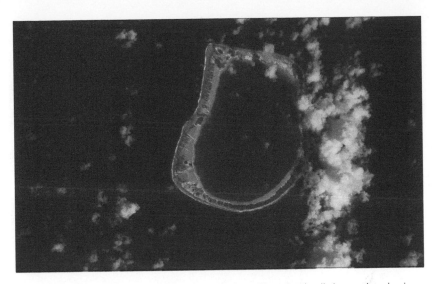

Two thousand miles to the southeast of Canton, Tuanake Atoll shows the classic cone shape of the volcano it once was, revealing how little actual land there was for pilots to spot as they passed over.
Courtesy Wikimedia Commons

DID YOU KNOW?

Canton Island is one of hundreds of small islands in the central and southern Pacific called atolls. An atoll is a ring-shaped coral reef island (or a group of such islands), often with a lagoon in the middle. They are formed from the buildup of lava from underwater volcanoes and from the growth of coral around it. Over eons, eroded limestone from decayed coral washes up on the island as sand.

Five years before Rickenbacker's Pacific mission, Amelia Earhart and Fred Noonan were making their historic flight around the world. They needed to find an even smaller atoll, Howland Island, on their way from New Guinea to Hawaii. As had Rickenbacker's pilot, Earhart established radio contact but was unable to receive a bearing. Unlike Rickenbacker and his crew, she and Noonan were never seen again.

10

DESCENT AND LANDING

August 1945 to July 23, 1973

"To me the freedom to work . . . is the most gratifying experience in my life."

—Eddie Rickenbacker[1]

T HE WAR was over, but Rickenbacker kept fighting—for his company, his country, and his values. When the Civil Aeronautics Board opened up Eastern's territory to competing airlines, Rickenbacker objected. "We pioneered that route—they're our cities and that's our market."[2] As the country entered the **Cold War** against its former ally, the Soviet Union, he spoke out forcefully against the "sinister, fanatical, enslaving creed" of **communism**.[3] Most of all, he railed against what he saw as the loss of America's central values: hard work and self-reliance. "Too many parents teach their children that the world owes them a living and that they have no debts toward society," he complained.[4]

Hard work. It still defined him. At sixty years old, Rickenbacker still rose as early as three o'clock in the morning (and no later than five) to read letters and reports before heading into the office. He still

Giving speeches and radio addresses was a regular habit for Rickenbacker by 1946.
Courtesy of Auburn University Libraries Special Collections and Archives

worked most weekends and never asked anyone to do anything he wouldn't first do himself. But he was demanding of others and critical of anyone who expected to get comfort and security without working for them. In one speech, he said Americans "did not suffer enough," that they wanted to live "painlessly from the cradle to the grave."[5] Rickenbacker knew from experience that hardship and suffering make a person strong. "Learning the hard way is still the best way," he said.[6]

Rickenbacker worked hard out of habit but also to serve others. He was convinced that air transport and air travel—his life's work—would benefit the world by bringing people closer together and by promoting greater understanding among nations.[7] The veteran of two world wars believed the airplane could be "an Angel of Peace."[8]

Rickenbacker worked hard so he could support his family, too. It gave him satisfaction—"more satisfaction than you will ever know," he wrote his son Bill[9]—to give his sons the things he never had: a childhood free from adult responsibility, an education of the highest quality. Bill, especially, thrived in the classroom. He excelled at languages, literature, and piano, and went on to graduate from Harvard. The self-taught mechanic's son was an Ivy Leaguer, just like those cocky cadets at Issoudun so many years before.

It made Rickenbacker proud. But there could be awkward moments, too, as when the father replied to the son's letter, "Gosh! You certainly get me down with your great, big words. I have to go to the dictionary to look up the meaning of them, to say nothing of your French quotations."[10] The busy airline executive always made time to write his sons when they were away at boarding school or college. And he was always generous with advice. He wanted them to benefit from his hard-won experience. As he told Bill, "I do not want you to learn the hard way as has been my experience."[11] (Apparently, the hard way was not *always* the best way.)

Dave was more like his father, interested in machines and working with his hands. He served as a marine in the Pacific during the war, which also made his father proud. In the 1950s, Rickenbacker hired Dave to run a working ranch he had purchased in Texas. Eddie and Adelaide stayed there whenever he could get away from New York. And Bill, who was then training to be a pilot at a nearby air force base, visited on weekends. "We all had many happy hours together," Rickenbacker recalled.[12]

Rickenbacker retired from Eastern Air Lines in stages—and only reluctantly. In 1953 he gave up his title as president but still held the controls. Five years later, he lost his position as general manager, but as chairman of the board continued to pull the strings. Five years after that, the company was still turning profits, but Captain Eddie's one-man rule was increasingly out of place in a large modern corporation. The Eastern board of directors forced him to step down. After sixty years in the work force, twenty-eight of them at the controls of Eastern Air Lines, the seventy-three-year-old Rickenbacker was out of work. What would he do with himself now?

He decided to publish his autobiography to inspire the young people of America and "make them aware of their destiny and the American way of life."[13] He hired a **ghostwriter** by the name of Booton Herndon, then spent more than a year gathering his papers, making recordings, and meeting with Herndon. The book sold a quarter of a million copies in its first year in print. Americans were as eager as ever to hear the story of the man who mastered speed on land and air, built an airline, and cheated death so many times.

Eddie and Adelaide continued to travel as much as they were able. On a trip to East Asia and the South Pacific, Rickenbacker made a brief stop at Canton Island, the atoll that had eluded him and his crew on the Pacific mission. He told a reporter that with modern equipment it wasn't at all hard to find. "We could see the beacon for seventy-five miles before we reached it," he said.[14] On a trip to North Africa and Italy, Eddie had another brush with death when their car was cut off by a reckless driver. Eddie escaped unharmed, but Adelaide was hospitalized with painful injuries.

When Eddie's feats were still just dreams ...
Courtesy of Auburn University Libraries Special Collections and Archives

been a part of so many of the twentieth century's defining events and technologies. He "always did his best and expected others to do the same," said one. He was "a man whose genius lives in every screaming engine and lifting, glistening wing," said another.[16]

Eddie would have claimed his life was an example of the American Dream. A true patriot, he always gave the greater credit to his country. "Where," he asked, "is there another land in the world where a young man can come from the wrong side of the railroad tracks"—or from a "little house" on Livingston Avenue—"and graduate into a relative position of leadership and affluence because of the very freedoms, liberties, and opportunities that this land offers?"[17]

Eddie did grow up in an era of abundant American opportunity for white boys and men of all classes, yet without his intense determination, his many accomplishments would never have been realized. He made up for a lack of high school and college education with an ongoing resolve to teach himself. He took a correspondence course, found mentors, hustled, and made a study of anything and everything that could advance his career. "I have always had an insatiable desire to learn," he told his hometown newspaper as he neared retirement.[18]

"Whatever happiness may mean to others," Rickenbacker told another publication, "to me the freedom to work, which is the basis of our American heritage, is the most gratifying experience in my life."[19] For whatever it was he was doing—carrying trays of hot glass, engraving headstones, troubleshooting temperamental automobiles, pushing race cars to ever faster speeds, shooting down enemy planes, selling his own and GM's automobiles, building an airline into greatness—he felt it was his privilege to "have been able to make some tangible contribution to the welfare of my country and my fellow man."[20]

Eddie Rickenbacker made a name for himself by *giving* of himself—with an energy seldom equaled in the history of his country.

DID YOU KNOW?

Rickenbacker International Airport is one of three airports in Columbus. Lockbourne Air Force Base, established in 1942, was renamed Rickenbacker Air Force Base in 1974. It was almost shut down in the 1990s due to budget cuts but gained new life as a major international freight airport during the following decade. Today Rickenbacker International Airport offers a limited number of passenger flights, too.

Timeline

Oct. 8, 1890
>Born in Columbus, Ohio

1893
>Rickenbacker family moves to the "little house" at 1334 Livingston Avenue

Aug. 26, 1904
>Eddie's father, William Rickenbacker, dies after thirty-nine days in a coma

Oct. 1906
>Fails to qualify for Vanderbilt Cup race on Long Island, New York

1907
>Goes to work for Columbus Buggy Company

June 9, 1910
>Competes in first dirt-track automobile race in Red Oak, Iowa

May 30, 1911
>Competes in first Indianapolis 500, driving the middle miles for Lee Frayer

July 4, 1914
>Wins Sioux City 100-mile race

Nov. 30, 1916
>Wins the 150-mile Championship Sweepstakes in Los Angeles, the last race of his career

June–Aug. 1917
>Serves as chauffeur for General Pershing and other military officials "somewhere in France"

Oct. 1917

Completes flight school and reports to Issoudun as chief construction engineer

Mar. 28, 1918

Makes the 94th Aero Squadron's first patrol over the line under the command of Major Raoul Lufbery

June 12, 1918

Becomes an ace after his fifth "victory" of May 30 is confirmed

Sept. 24, 1918

Made commander of the 94th Hat-in-the-Ring Squadron

Nov. 11, 1918

Flies over No Man's Land on Armistice Day

Feb.–July 1919

Welcomed home as a hero in New York, Columbus, Los Angeles, and other cities

Jan. 1922

The Rickenbacker Six automobile, "A Car Worthy of Its Name," goes on sale to the public

Sept. 16, 1922

Marries Adelaide Frost Durant; takes a seven-week honeymoon to Europe

Nov. 1925

Establishes the short-lived Florida Airways with Hat-in-the-Ring buddy Reed Chambers

Nov. 1, 1927

Buys the Indianapolis Motor Speedway for $700,000 with help of a bank loan

Nov. 6, 1930

Awarded the Congressional Medal of Honor for heroism in the air over Billy, France, September 25, 1918

Jan. 1, 1935

Made general manager of Eastern Air Lines

Dec. 1935

Takes a family vacation to Europe; tours Nazi air force facilities

Apr. 19, 1938

Buys Eastern Air Lines from General Motors with $3.5 million loan

Feb. 26, 1941

Suffers serious injuries in EAL Flight 21 crash in woods outside Atlanta

Mar.–Oct. 1942

Makes two tours of inspection for the United States Army Air Forces, first in the United States, then in the United Kingdom

Oct. 21–Nov. 13, 1942

Survives twenty-three days adrift in life raft in the Pacific

Apr. 27–Aug. 3, 1943

Makes a three-month, 55,000-mile world mission to a dozen different nations in South America, Africa, Asia, and Europe

Aug. 1945

Captain Eddie, a feature movie about Rickenbacker's life and Pacific ordeal, is released

Nov. 1945

Sells the Indianapolis Motor Speedway for $750,000

Mar. 31, 1946

Eddie's mother, Lizzie Rickenbacker, dies at age eighty-two in the California home Eddie provided for her

Jan. 1, 1957

Rides, with Adelaide, as grand marshal in the Tournament of Roses Parade in Pasadena, California

Dec. 31, 1963

Officially retires from Eastern Air Lines

1967

Publishes autobiography, *Rickenbacker*

July 23, 1973

Dies in Zurich, Switzerland

1995

The United States Postal Service issues a postage stamp in honor of Edward V. Rickenbacker

Captain Eddie's Advice to Young People, 1953

I learned very early that I needed a plan of living to attain my one great ambition—to be a good American. Now this plan of mine may not fit everybody. But with the hope that it might help you, I'd like to tell you about it.

1. Prayer . . . is a very real source of power. I know it has saved my life more times than I can remember.

2. Believe in the principles of your religion, in people and your country. Believe in life and particularly in yourself.

3. Honesty: Be honest with yourself first, because if you are, you will have to be honest with everyone else.

4. Work: The freedom to choose the type of work you like best is one of our greatest blessings.

5. Share Your Blessings: If God has given [to] us abundantly, he has also given us responsibilities to share our abundance with those less fortunate.

6. Save: Only through saving can we build our resources to help us in the future.

7. Citizenship: Vote when you become of age. . . . Your vote and the vote of every American is needed to keep us free.

8. Love Your Country: And that love means love for every American, wherever he comes from, whatever his color, however he worships.

Glossary

aerodrome: airport or airfield, especially in France in World War I

agency: a place to automobiles, a dealership

airship: an aircraft that moves with the power of an engine but flies using lighter-than-air gas, hydrogen or helium. (Blimps, Zeppelins, and observation balloons are examples of airships.)

Allies: during World War I, those nations—France, Great Britain, and Russia—that joined together to fight against the Central Powers, led by Germany. The United States and other countries later joined the Allied powers. During World War II, the chief Allied powers were Great Britain, France, the Soviet Union, the United States, and China.

antiaircraft: the guns or the shells used to attack an enemy airplane

apprentice: a young worker learning a trade from a skilled employer

assembly line: a series of workers who individually perform a single task in the construction of an automobile (or another product). The automobile moves down the line to each worker, who completes his or her task before it moves down to the next worker.

aviation: the flying of an aircraft. (People who fly aircraft are aviators.)

ballyhoo: loud, showy, attention-grabbing publicity

bankruptcy: when an individual is declared by law as unable to pay back debts. (The individual goes to court to eliminate or reduce all or part of his or her debts.)

barracks: a building or group of buildings used to house soldiers

biplane: an airplane—or aeroplane, as they wrote in 1918—with two sets of wings, one on top of the other. (A wing is a kind of *plane*, a simple machine that deflects air down in order to lift the aircraft up. In the early days, when speed was not great, two sets of planes—wings—were often better than one.)

campaign: an organized military action designed to achieve a strategic goal in a war

castor oil: vegetable oil made from pressed castor beans, the only oil that could be used in the Nieuport 28's rotary engine

chauffeur: a driver of an automobile. (The word comes from the French for "someone who heats up." The person who stoked a steam engine to keep it going was called the *chauffeur*, and the first automobiles were run by steam engines. Later the term was expanded to mean anyone who drove any kind of automobile.)

circuit: an established series of performances or races in a given time frame or season

class prejudice: when members of a higher class discriminate against those of a lower class. (Social class is the division of society into groups based on how much money and/or education people have.)

Cold War: an intense rivalry between the United States and the Soviet Union in the years between 1947 and 1991. The two countries never went directly to war, but the tension became so great that many worried it might lead to nuclear war.

coma: a deep state of unconsciousness when a person can neither move nor respond but is not dead

communism: a form of government in which the government plans and controls the economy: what will be produced, who will perform which jobs, and how much each person will be paid

credit: the trust a customer has earned that allows him to obtain a product before paying for it

dehydration: the loss of water in the body

delirium: a disturbed, feverish state of mind, often with hallucinations

devious: sneaky, underhanded

distress call: a signal or communication in an emergency designed to get help quickly

eulogist: a speaker who gives a speech at a funeral about the person who has died

executive: a senior manager in a large company

forced landing: emergency landing of an aircraft in a field or other open space

fringe benefit: a bonus on top of one's regular salary or wages

ghostwriter: an author who is hired to write a book for someone else who will get credit for it

hangars: large buildings used to house airplanes

hoodlum: a street tough or gang member

hops: flowers of the hop plant used for flavoring beer

hustle: to work quickly; also to be pushy or sneaky in order to get what you want

infirmary: a clinic or hospital within a military encampment

internal combustion engine: a motor that runs on gasoline or similar fuel. (See "pistons.")

Kraut: a degrading term for a person of German heritage. (This comes from the fact that Germans were known for eating sauerkraut.)

Lafayette Escadrille: a unit of volunteer American pilots who flew for France during World War I before the United States entered the war. It served from April 20, 1916, to February 18, 1918.

lathe: a machine for shaping metal by rotating the item against a cutting blade

latrines: outhouses or toilets used in a military encampment

machinist: a person who works with machine tools to cut and shape metal for engine parts or for other metal products

market: an area of the economy in which a type of good (in this case, automobiles) are bought and sold

memorabilia: items connected with an important historical figure

mentor: an experienced and trusted adviser and teacher

morale: confidence, enthusiasm, and discipline of a group; how they feel about themselves and their work

No Man's Land: during World War I, the territory between the trenches of the Allies on one side and the Germans on the other, a couple miles wide in some places or a couple hundred yards in others

pistons: solid cylinders fitted inside cylindrical chambers, connected to crankshafts that drive them up or down with each spark-ignition of an internal combustion engine (the up and down motion powers the turning of the wheels)

pit: the place beside the track where racing teams refuel, change tires, and make repairs. (Stopping in the pit to refuel, change tires, etc., is called a pit stop.)

play hooky: to skip school

pneumonia: inflammation of the lung caused by infection

profit: money gained by a business

pursuit pilot: a fighter pilot who battles enemy pilots for control of the skies

reformatory: reform school; an alternative to prison for young criminals

replica: a model or copy

Sam Browne belts: brown leather belts that wrap around the waist but have a second strap that goes from the left hip over the right shoulder, worn only by officers

sector: an area of military operations

squalls: small, localized rainstorms

tailspin: when an airplane dives directly to the earth in a spiral rotation

the Channel: the body of water that separates England from France, 21 miles at its narrowest and 150 miles at its widest

transcontinental: across the continent

transcripts: typed or printed copies of original documents

tycoon: a wealthy, powerful person in business or industry. (Vanderbilt made his money in steamboats and railroads.)

Victrola: a popular brand of phonograph, or record player, in the early twentieth century

wage laborer: someone who does hard physical work and is paid by the hour

western front: refers to the part of World War I that took place in France as opposed to the part in Russia in the east and other fronts in the south and elsewhere

wingman: a pilot whose aircraft is positioned behind and to the side of a leading aircraft and pilot; the junior partner in a pair of combat pilots

withal: in addition, all the same, nevertheless

Acknowledgments

I am grateful for the assistance of many librarians and archivists in the research of this book. Scott Caputo, *primus inter pares*, responded to more than a dozen email inquiries and passed along numerous digital scans from his post at Columbus Metro Library, Local History and Genealogy. Rebecca Jewett and her staff at the Rare Books and Manuscripts Library at Ohio State University hosted me on four occasions and filled orders for scans of more than 250 pages of transcripts. Shawna Woodard of the Dayton Metro Library, Tom Moosbrugger of the Public Library of Cincinnati and Hamilton County, Hang Nguyen of the State Historical Society of Iowa, Lauren B. of the Benson Ford Research Center at the Henry Ford, and Chris Cottrill of the Smithsonian Institution all responded to specific queries at key moments in my search.

John Varner of Auburn University Special Collections and Archives was especially helpful responding to my inquiries and giving me access to the abundance of photos in the university's Eddie Rickenbacker Collection. The same is true of Lily Birkhimer of the Ohio History Center, who led me to several crucial images for the early chapters. Brian Balsley turned my vision for a pair of Eddie Rickenbacker maps into reality, making them appealing and stimulating to look at.

I am grateful for Ohio University Press having the confidence to hire me for this project and for being supportive every step of the way. Rick Huard and Sally Welch anticipated my questions with their thorough publishing guidelines and answered any others with alacrity and aplomb. Michelle Houts saved me from making unforced errors and pushed me gently to improve my writing. My two expert readers also provided essential feedback that allowed me to correct inaccuracies and to sharpen my thinking about Eddie Rickenbacker. Chiquita Babb reviewed the entire manuscript with impressive thoroughness and attention to detail. Beth Pratt produced a book that will make me proud to pull off the shelf and hand to a child.

I am indebted to Tracy Vonder Brink and Rebecca Barone, my nonfiction critique partners, as well as my monthly critique group, Kathy W., Kathy M., Michele, Henry, Josephine, Frank, Amy, and Pam, for giving me feedback on drafts of almost every chapter in this book.

Thank you, Erin and Benjamin, for the inspiration you provide every day, just by being yourselves. Thank you, Sue, most of all, for giving me the love and support I need to do this work I enjoy so much.

Notes

Author's Note

1. Ralph De Palma, quoted in W. David Lewis, *Eddie Rickenbacker: An American Hero in the Twentieth Century* (Baltimore: Johns Hopkins University Press, 2005), 63.

Chapter One: Black Sheep of the Family

1. Edward V. Rickenbacker, *Life Story* 2:408, Eddie Rickenbacker Papers, 1915–72, SPEC.RARE.MS.AMER.18, Rare Books and Manuscripts Library of the Ohio State University, Columbus.

2. Ibid., 545.

3. Ibid., 671.

4. Edward V. Rickenbacker, *Rickenbacker: An Autobiography* (Englewood Cliffs, NJ: Prentice-Hall, 1967), 5.

5. Lewis, *Eddie Rickenbacker*, 6.

6. Rickenbacker, *Life Story* 1:3, 10.

7. Ibid., 13.

8. Rickenbacker, *Rickenbacker*, 9.

9. Ibid., 5; Rickenbacker, *Life Story* 1:8.

10. Rickenbacker, *Life Story* 1:15.

11. Ibid., 7.

12. Ibid., 34.

13. Ibid., 7.

14. Ibid., 14.

15. Ibid., 10–11.

16. Ibid., 34–35.

17. Rickenbacker, *Rickenbacker*, 8.

18. "Gaines Claims He Hit in Self-Defense," *Ohio State Journal,* July 21, 1904. See also *Columbus Evening Dispatch,* July 18, 19, 23, and August 2, 5, 26, 1904.

19. Rickenbacker, *Rickenbacker*, 18.

Chapter Two: Man of the House

1. Edward V. Rickenbacker, "You Can't Get Something for Nothing," *Statements*, Eddie Rickenbacker Papers, 1915–72.

2. Rickenbacker, *Life Story* 1:51.

3. Ibid., 53.

4. Rickenbacker, *Rickenbacker*, 29–31; Rickenbacker, *Life Story* 1:55–56.

Chapter Three: Moving Up in the World

1. Rickenbacker, *Rickenbacker*, 43.

2. Rickenbacker, *Life Story* 1:60.

3. Ibid., 61.

4. T. J. Stiles, *The First Tycoon: The Epic Life of Cornelius Vanderbilt* (New York: Vintage, 2010).

5. Rickenbacker, *Rickenbacker*, 39.

6. Ibid., 43.

7. Rickenbacker, *Life Story* 1:66–67.

8. Ibid., 71.

9. Ibid., 81.

10. Walter J. Boyne, *Aces in Command: Fighter Pilots as Combat Leaders* (Washington, DC: Brassey's, 2001), 16.

Chapter Four: King of the Dirt-Track Racers

1. Rickenbacker, *Life Story* 2:510.

2. Henry Ford, with Samuel Crowther, *My Life and Work* (New York: Doubleday, Page, 1922), 37.

3. Rickenbacker, *Rickenbacker*, 52.

4. Rickenbacker, *Life Story* 2:510.

5. Rickenbacker, *Rickenbacker*, 57.

6. Ibid., 60.

7. "Rickenbacker in Duesenberg Wins 300-Mile Race," *Motor Age*, July 9, 1914, 9–10.

8. Lewis, *Eddie Rickenbacker*, 70.

9. Rickenbacker, *Life Story* 1:117.

10. "Great Drivers to Pilot Maxwells: Barney Oldfield, Billy Carlson and Eddie Rickenbacker," *Hartford Courant*, March 14, 1915, z7.

11. A. G. Waddell, "Resta's Generalship Won Vanderbilt," *Automobile*, March 18, 1915, 512–13.

12. Edward V. Rickenbacker, "When a Man Faces Death," 15, Eddie Rickenbacker Papers, 1915–72.

13. "With Grantland Rice—Coca-Cola Hour," May 21, 1930, *Broadcasts* 1, Eddie Rickenbacker Papers, 1915–72.

14. Finis Farr, *Rickenbacker's Luck: An American Life* (Boston: Houghton Mifflin, 1979), 22.

15. Ibid.

16. Lewis, *Eddie Rickenbacker*, 85.

17. Rickenbacker, *Life Story* 1:139.

18. A. S. Blakely, "Aitken Wins Every Race," *Indianapolis Star*, September 10, 1916, A1.

19. Rickenbacker, *Life Story* 1:139.

20. Ibid., 140.

21. Ibid., 141.

22. "Eddie Rickenbacher Is Here for Auto Races," *Los Angeles Times*, November 6, 1916, 19.

Chapter Five: Hat in the Ring

1. Rickenbacker, *Rickenbacker*, 89.

2. "Flying Corps of Daring Racing Drivers Plan if War Comes," *New York Times*, February 18, 1917, xx2.

3. "Rickenbacker Is Driver of Pershing's Car," *Nashville Tennessean*, August 2, 1917, 10.

4. Rickenbacker, *Rickenbacker*, 89.

5. Rickenbacker, "When a Man Faces Death," 20.

6. "Alone? Yes, To Be Sure! Candidate Takes Seat in Plane All by Himself," *Cincinnati Enquirer*, July 21, 1918, 14; Rickenbacker, *Rickenbacker*, 90.

7. John F. Ross, *Enduring Courage: Ace Pilot Eddie Rickenbacker and the Dawn of the Age of Speed* (New York: St. Martin's Press, 2014), 121.

8. Lewis, *Eddie Rickenbacker*, 105.

9. Rickenbacker, *Rickenbacker*, 92.

10. Reed M. Chambers, interview by Kenneth W. Leish, October 1960, file 146.34-26, Oral History Research Office, Butler Library, Columbia University,

New York, https://clio.columbia.edu/catalog/4073980, quoted in Robert J. Serling, *From the Captain to the Colonel: An Informal History of Eastern Airlines* (New York: Dial Press, 1980), 90.

11. Anonymous aviator, quoted in C. V. Glines, "Charmed Life of Captain Eddie Rickenbacker," *Aviation History*, August 23, 2012, https://www.historynet.com/charmed-life-of-captain-eddie-rickenbacker-january-99-aviation-history-feature.htm.

12. Chambers, interview by Kenneth W. Leish, quoted in Serling, *From the Captain to the Colonel*, 90.

13. Ross, *Enduring Courage*, 127–29.

14. Rickenbacker, *Rickenbacker*, 92.

15. Ibid., 94–95.

16. Ibid., 95.

17. Boyne, *Aces in Command*, 34.

18. Captain Edward V. Rickenbacker, *Fighting the Flying Circus* (New York: Frederick A. Stokes, 1919), 10.

19. Captain Paul H. Walters, quoted in Bert Frandsen, *Hat in the Ring: The Birth of American Air Power in the Great War* (Washington, DC: Smithsonian Books, 2003), 78.

Chapter Six: Ace of Aces

1. Tom Trueblood, "Gimpers Flew Cans to 'Pink Teas' in WWI Where They 'Piqued' Boche," *Columbus Citizen-Journal*, October 3, 1967.

2. Rickenbacker, *Fighting the Flying Circus*, 26.

3. Ibid., 27.

4. Howard Johnson, *Wings Over Brooklands: The Story of the Birthplace of British Aviation* (Surrey: Whittet Books, 1981), 49–50.

5. Tom Fennessy, "Adventure Filled Life of Ace," *Columbus Dispatch*, July 23, 1973.

6. Rickenbacker, *Fighting the Flying Circus*, 132.

7. Hamilton Coolidge, quoted in Charles Woolley, *The Hat in the Ring Gang: The Combat History of the 94th Aero Squadron in World War I* (Atglen, PA: Schiffer Military History, 2001), 118.

8. Rickenbacker, *Fighting the Flying Circus*, 132.

9. J. L. Maloney, "Comrade of '18 Finds Rick the Leader of Yore," *Chicago Daily Tribune*, January 24, 1943, 3; on Rickenbacker's mental transformation: Lewis, *Eddie Rickenbacker*, 198, and Ross, *Enduring Courage*, 250.

10. Frandsen, *Hat in the Ring*, 196.

11. Rickenbacker, *Life Story* 2:516.

12. Chambers, interview by Kenneth W. Leish, quoted in Ezra Bowen, *Knights of the Air* (New York: Time-Life Books, 1980), 174; Ross, *Enduring Courage*, 249.

13. Douglas Campbell, quoted in Woolley, *The Hat in the Ring Gang*, 40.

14. Rickenbacker, *Life Story* 2:523.

15. Description of final patrol: Rickenbacker, *Rickenbacker*, 135.

16. Rickenbacker, *Fighting the Flying Circus*, 360.

17. Rickenbacker, "When a Man Faces Death," 31.

Chapter Seven: Grounded

1. "Rickenbacker Reports on America's Fighter Planes," September 4, 1942, *Broadcasts* 1.

2. "Baker and 600 Guests at Dinner to Rickenbacker Follow Him in Saluting," *St. Louis Post-Dispatch*, February 4, 1919.

3. "Columbus Bids Proud Welcome to War-Celebrated Fellow-Citizen," *Columbus Dispatch*, February 17, 1919, 1.

4. Rickenbacker, *Rickenbacker*, 66.

5. Rickenbacker, *Life Story* 2:468–69.

6. "Will Welcome Ace Today," *Los Angeles Times*, June 21, 1919, 111; Rickenbacker, *Rickenbacker*, 141.

7. Ralph Kramer, *Indianapolis Motor Speedway: 100 Years of Racing* (Iola, WI: Krause Publications, 2009), 84; Rickenbacker, *Life Story* 1:232.

8. "Four Aces Back with Total of 40 Hun Scalps," *Indianapolis Star*, February 1, 1919, 1.

9. Beverly Rae Kimes, "Hat in the Ring: The Rickenbacker," *Automobile Quarterly*, Fall 1975, 424.

10. Transcontinental crossings: Lewis, *Eddie Rickenbacker*, 246–48, 250–51, 256; Rickenbacker, *Life Story* 2:413–28; *Ohio State Journal*, August 4, 1920; May 21, 1921; May 27, 1921; Columbus Biography R, box 1, F9 Rickenbacker, E. (25), Local History Notebooks, Columbus Metropolitan Library, Columbus, OH.

11. Don Rogers, "Rickenbacker—Air Lines Wizard," *Scribner's Commentator*, June 1941, 50.

12. Walter Kiernan, "Rickenbacker Went to Work at Age of 12," *Columbus Dispatch*, November 11, 1942, 17.

13. Florida Airways data: Lewis, *Eddie Rickenbacker*, 288–89; Rickenbacker, *Life Story* 1:294.

14. Rickenbacker, *Rickenbacker*, 149.

15. Model T datum: John Rae, *The American Automobile Industry* (Woodbridge, CT: Twayne, 1985), 38; Sloan, quoted in William Pelfrey, *Billy, Alfred, and General Motors* (New York: AMACOM, 2006), 252.

Chapter Eight: At the Controls

1. Rickenbacker, "My Constitution," *Statements*, 1935.

2. "Aviation Comes of Age," Century of Flight, undated, http://www.century-of-flight.freeola.com/Aviation%20history/coming%20of%20age/splash.htm.

3. Serling, *From the Captain to the Colonel*, 125.

4. Farr, *Rickenbacker's Luck*, 178.

5. "Flight Makes Record: Eastern Airline Flies 22 Persons, Non-Stop, for 1,231 Miles," *New York Times*, May 17, 1937, 8; "Merrill Will Fly to Aid Ellsworth: Crack Eastern Air Lines' Pilot Succeeds Thaw as Man to Take Relief Plane South," *New York Times*, December 11, 1935, 16; "Basketball Star Misses Bus, Then Captain Rickenbacker Comes to His Aid. Plane Whisks Boy, 15, to Capital for Game," *New York Times*, March 15, 1936, 34.

6. Rickenbacker, "My Constitution," 1935, *Statements*.

7. Serling, *From the Captain to the Colonel*, 128, 134.

8. Rickenbacker, "When a Man Faces Death," 48.

9. Ibid., 50.

10. Rickenbacker, *Rickenbacker*, 238.

11. Ibid., 241.

12. Ibid., 243.

13. Rickenbacker, "When a Man Faces Death," 56–57.

14. Rickenbacker, *Rickenbacker*, 247.

15. Ibid., 249.

Chapter Nine: Mayday

1. "Rickenbacker," in *Time: Great People of the 20th Century* (New York: Time Books, 1996), 114.

2. Rickenbacker, *Rickenbacker,* 250; Rickenbacker, *Life Story* 1:276.

3. Lewis, *Eddie Rickenbacker,* 142.

4. Edward V. Rickenbacker, "Acceptance Speech, Capital University," July 31, 1945, *Speeches and Addresses* 3, Eddie Rickenbacker Papers, 1915–72.

5. Lewis, *Eddie Rickenbacker,* 389.

6. "Keep Us Out of War," September 26, 1939, *Broadcasts* 1.

7. "Rickenbacker, 4 Months in Hospital, Back; He Will Resume His Airline Post on Monday," *New York Times,* June 26, 1941, 24.

8. Rickenbacker, *Rickenbacker,* 284.

9. Ibid., 272.

10. Ibid., 277.

11. "Rickenbacker Reports on War in the Air," August 30, 1942, *Broadcasts* 1.

12. Rickenbacker, *Rickenbacker,* 279.

13. Captain Edward V. Rickenbacker, *Seven Came Through: Rickenbacker's Full Story* (Garden City: Doubleday, Doran, 1943), 38.

14. Lieutenant James C. Whittaker, *We Thought We Heard the Angels Sing* (New York: E. P. Dutton, 1943), 93, 102.

15. Rickenbacker, *Rickenbacker,* 324.

16. Hans Christian Adamson, *Eddie Rickenbacker* (New York: Macmillan, 1946), 304.

17. Robert L. O'Connell, "Captain Eddie's Second World War," *MHQ: Quarterly Journal of Military History* 17, no. 1 (September 2004): 75; Lewis, *Eddie Rickenbacker,* 442.

18. Rickenbacker, "Am I My Brother's Keeper?," May 17, 1944, *Speeches and Addresses* 3.

19. "Rickenbacker Sets Detroit Goals in Blunt Talk to War Workers, *New York Times,* January 23, 1943, 8.

20. Farr, *Rickenbacker's Luck,* 247.

Chapter Ten: Descent and Landing

1. Rickenbacker, "What Do You Mean by Happiness?," Ladies Home Journal Symposium, 1933, *Statements.*

2. Serling, *From the Captain to the Colonel,* 212.

3. Rickenbacker, "Our Duty to Understand, Believe, and Work," February 25, 1948, *Speeches and Addresses* 4.

4. Ibid.

5. Rickenbacker, "America Must Return to Fundamentals," December 12, 1946, *Speeches and Addresses* 3.

6. Rickenbacker, *Life Story* 2:671.

7. Ibid., 609.

8. Edward V. Rickenbacker (as told to Gardner Harding), "50,000 Planes Can't Be Wrong," *Collier's*, April 29, 1939, 61.

9. Edward V. Rickenbacker, *From Father to Son: The Letters of Captain Eddie Rickenbacker to His Son William, from Boyhood to Manhood*, ed. William F. Rickenbacker (New York: Walker, 1970), 63.

10. Ibid., 36.

11. Ibid., 74.

12. Rickenbacker, *Rickenbacker*, 419.

13. Johnny Jones, "Rickenbacker Visit Stirs Memories of Other Days," *Columbus Dispatch*, October 17, 1967, 3B.

14. Lewis, *Eddie Rickenbacker*, 531.

15. Rickenbacker, "Let's Appreciate Our Heritage," November 3, 1949, *Speeches and Addresses* 4.

16. "Capt. Eddie Honored in Renaming of Base," *Columbus Dispatch*, May 19, 1974, 1A.

17. Rickenbacker, "Let's Appreciate Our Heritage," 1949, *Speeches and Addresses* 4.

18. James Kilgallen, "Rickenbacker Believes Security Kills Initiative," *Columbus Dispatch*, June 19, 1955, E1.

19. Rickenbacker, "What Do You Mean by Happiness?," 1933, *Statements*.

20. Ibid.

Bibliography

Books

Adamson, Hans Christian. *Eddie Rickenbacker.* New York: Macmillan, 1946.

Barrett, Richard E. *Aviation in Columbus.* Charleston: Arcadia Publishing, 2012.

———. *Columbus: 1860–1910.* Charleston: Arcadia, 2005.

Bowen, Ezra. *Knights of the Air.* New York: Time-Life Books, 1980.

Boyne, Walter J. *Aces in Command: Fighter Pilots as Combat Leaders.* Washington, DC: Brassey's, 2001.

Buckley, Harold. *Squadron 95.* New York: Arno Press, 1972. Originally published as *Squadron 95: An Intimate History of the 95th Squadron First American Flying Squadron to Go to the Front in the War of 1914–1918.* Paris: Obelisk Press, 1933.

Farr, Finis. *Rickenbacker's Luck: An American Life.* Boston: Houghton Mifflin, 1979.

Flink, James J. *America Adopts the Automobile: 1895–1910.* Cambridge: MIT Press, 1970.

Ford, Henry, with Samuel Crowther. *My Life and Work.* New York: Doubleday, Page, 1922.

Frandsen, Bert. *Hat in the Ring: The Birth of American Air Power in the Great War.* Washington, DC: Smithsonian Books, 2003.

Johnson, Howard. *Wings Over Brooklands: The Story of the Birthplace of British Aviation.* Surrey: Whittet Books, 1981.

Kimes, Beverly Rae, and Harry C. Clarke. *Standard Catalogue of American Cars, 1805–1942,* 3rd ed. Iola, WI: Krause Publications, 1996, 363–65, 564–65, 612–13.

Kramer, Ralph. *Indianapolis Motor Speedway: 100 Years of Racing.* Iola, WI: Krause Publications, 2009.

Langewiesche, Wolfgang. *Stick and Rudder: An Explanation of the Art of Flying.* New York: McGraw Hill, 1944.

Lentz, Ed. *Columbus: The Story of a City.* Charleston, SC: Arcadia, 2003, 43–46, 61–65, 83–113.

Lewis, W. David. *Eddie Rickenbacker: An American Hero in the Twentieth Century.* Baltimore: Johns Hopkins University Press, 2005.

Pelfrey, William. *Billy, Alfred, and General Motors.* New York: AMACOM, 2006.

Rae, John. *The American Automobile Industry.* Woodbridge, CT: Twayne, 1985.

Rickenbacker, Captain Edward V. *Fighting the Flying Circus.* New York: Frederick A. Stokes, 1919.

———. *Seven Came Through: Rickenbacker's Full Story.* Garden City, NY: Doubleday, Doran, 1943.

Rickenbacker, Edward V. *From Father to Son: The Letters of Captain Eddie Rickenbacker to His Son William, from Boyhood to Manhood.* Edited by William F. Rickenbacker. New York: Walker, 1970.

———. *Rickenbacker: An Autobiography.* Englewood Cliffs, NJ: Prentice-Hall, 1967.

Rippley, La Vern J. *The Columbus Germans.* Indianapolis: Indiana German Heritage Society, 1998.

Ross, John F. *Enduring Courage: Ace Pilot Eddie Rickenbacker and the Dawn of the Age of Speed.* New York: St. Martin's Press, 2014.

Serling, Robert J. *From the Captain to the Colonel: An Informal History of Eastern Airlines.* New York: Dial Press, 1980.

Stiles, T. J. *The First Tycoon: The Epic Life of Cornelius Vanderbilt.* New York: Vintage, 2010.

Time: Great People of the 20th Century. New York: Time Books, 1996.

Whittaker, Lieutenant James C. *We Thought We Heard the Angels Sing.* New York: E. P. Dutton, 1943.

Woolley, Charles. *The Hat in the Ring Gang: The Combat History of the 94th Aero Squadron in World War I.* Atglen, PA: Schiffer Military History, 2001.

Articles

"Buggy Capital of the World." *Columbus Dispatch* (blog), July 29, 2015. https://www.dispatch.com/article/20150729/BLOGS/307299846.

Cook, Kevin L. "Flying Blind." *MHQ: Quarterly Journal of Military History* 20, no. 3 (September 2004): 76–83.

"Durable Man." *Time*, April 17, 1950, 24–27.

Glines, C. V. "Charmed Life of Captain Eddie Rickenbacker." *Aviation History*, August 23, 2012. https://www.historynet.com/charmed-life-of-captain-eddie-rickenbacker-january-99-aviation-history-feature.htm.

Helck, Peter. "Twenty-Four Hours to Go: A Saga of the Dirt Track Grinds in America." *Automobile Quarterly*, Summer 1966, 24–25, 56–67.

Kimes, Beverly Rae. "Hat in the Ring: The Rickenbacker." *Automobile Quarterly*, Fall 1975, 419–35.

———. "The Vanderbilt Cup Races, 1904–1910." *Automobile Quarterly*, Fall 1967, 185–99.

Lewis, W. David. "Historical Essay." In Rickenbacker, Captain Edward V., *Fighting the Flying Circus*. Chicago: R. R. Donnelly & Sons, 1997.

Marshall, Roy. "The Time Capsule: Eddie Rickenbacker: Race Driver to Fighting Ace." *Red Oak (IA) Express*, June 23, 2015. https://www.redoakexpress.com/content/time-capsule-eddie-rickenbacker-race-driver-fighting-ace.

O'Connell, Robert L. "Captain Eddie's Second World War." *MHQ: Quarterly Journal of Military History* 17, no. 1 (September 2004): 70–77.

Rickenbacker, E. V. "The New Transportation." *Ace*, July 1922, 9.

Rickenbacker, Edward V. (as told to Gardner Harding). "50,000 Planes Can't Be Wrong." *Collier's*, April 29, 1939, 9–10, 60–61.

Rogers, Don. "Rickenbacker—Air Lines Wizard." *Scribner's Commentator*, June 1941, 42–52.

Periodicals

Newspapers

Chicago Daily Tribune
Cincinnati Enquirer
Columbus Citizen-Journal
Columbus Dispatch
Columbus Evening Dispatch
Hartford Courant
Indianapolis Star
Los Angeles Times
Nashville Tennessean
New York Times
Ohio State Journal

St. Louis Post-Dispatch
Washington Post

Magazines and Journals

Automobile
Collier's
MHQ: Quarterly Journal of Military History
Motor Age
Road and Track
Scribner's Commentator

Archival Materials

Columbus Biography R, box 1, F9 Rickenbacker, E. Local History Notebooks. Columbus Metropolitan Library, Columbus, OH.
Eddie Rickenbacker Papers, 1915–72. Rare Books and Manuscripts Library of the Ohio State University Libraries, Columbus. SPEC.RARE.MS.AMER.18.
Reed M. Chambers, interview by Kenneth W. Leish, October 1960, file K146.34-26, Oral History Research Office, Butler Library, Columbia University, New York. https://clio.columbia.edu/catalog/4073980.

Online Sources

All online sources are listed within subject categories.

Eddie Rickenbacker

Rickenbacker, Edward V. "Eddie V. Rickenbacker WWI Diary." National Museum of the United States Air Force, March 2, 2018. https://www .nationalmuseum.af.mil/Visit/Museum-Exhibits/Fact-Sheets/Display /Article/1456443/eddie-v-rickenbacker-wwi-diary/.

Airplanes

"Aviation Comes of Age." Century of Flight, undated. http://www.century-of -flight.freeola.com/Aviation%20history/coming%20of%20age/splash .htm.

"Boeing B-17 Flying Fortress," "Caudron G.3," "Douglas DC-2," "Douglas DC-3," "Ford TriMotor," "Pitcairn Mailwing." Wikipedia. https://en.wikipedia.org.

"Nieuport 28." National Museum of the US Air Force. https://www.nationalmuseum.af.mil/Visit/Museum-Exhibits/Fact-Sheets/Display/Article/197403/nieuport-28/.

"Nieuport 28 Detail Photos." Military Aviation Archives. http://www.milavnarc.com/nieuport_28detail_photos.html.

"Spad XIII C.1." National Museum of the US Air Force. https://www.nationalmuseum.af.mil/Visit/Museum-Exhibits/Fact-Sheets/Display/Article/197399/spad-xiii.c1/.

Others

"1906 Vanderbilt Cup Race." Vanderbilt Cup Races. http://www.vanderbiltcupraces.com/races/story/1906_vanderbilt_cup_race.

"Ace Drummond," "Atolls," "Canton Island Airport," "Kanton Island," "Howland Island," "Mayday," "Rickenbacker International Airport." https://en.wikipedia.org.

"Atoll." National Geographic Society. https://www.nationalgeographic.org/encyclopedia/atoll/.

"Captain Eddie Rickenbacker Boyhood Home Replica." Motts Military Museum, undated. http://www.mottsmilitarymuseum.org/rickenbacker.html.

"History." German Village Society. https://germanvillage.com/about/history/.

"Indy Speedway History." Indy Speedway. http://indymotorspeedway.com/500hist.html.

"Knabenshue, A Roy: Daredevil/Promoter." The National Aviation Hall of Fame. https://www.nationalaviation.org/our-enshrinees/knabenshue-roy/.

"Memorial Day History." U.S. Department of Veterans Affairs, Office of Public and Intergovernmental Affairs, last updated July 20, 2015. https://www.va.gov/opa/speceven/memday/history.asp.

Sherman, Stephen. "The Hall of Fame of the Air: An Illustrated Newspaper Feature from 1935–1940," updated April 11, 2012. http://acepilots.com/wwi/hfa.html.

"Mayday and SOS." Infoplease, February 28, 2017. https://www.infoplease.com/askeds/mayday-and-sos.